Duties
of the Soul

The Role of Commandments
in Liberal Judaism

Edited with an Introduction by

NILES E. GOLDSTEIN

A N D

PETER S. KNOBEL

UAHC Press   ·   *New York*

To all those who seek

a serious approach to obligation

in contemporary Judaism

Library of Congress Cataloging-in-Publication Data
Duties of the soul : the role of commandments in Liberal Judaism /
edited by Niles E. Goldstein and Peter S. Knobel.
    p.   cm.
ISBN 0-8074-0653-8 (alk. paper)
1. Reform Judaism.   2. Commandments (Judaism)
I. Goldstein, Niles Elliot, 1966–   . II. Knobel, Peter S., 1943–   .
BM197.D87   1999
296.3'6—dc21   98-44395
                                                        CIP

This book is printed on acid-free paper.
Copyright © 1999 by the UAHC Press
Manufactured in the United States of America
10 9 8 7 6 5 4 3 2 1

Contents

Introduction   v

&ea; Part I: What Is Mitzvah?

1. Reform Judaism and Mitzvot: A Historical Overview   3
DANIEL M. BRONSTEIN

2. Back to the Future: On Rediscovering Commandments   19
ARNOLD JACOB WOLF

3. A Reform View of Mitzvot   28
ERIC H. YOFFIE

4. Recovering the Hidden Torah:
A Mystical Paradigm for Mitzvah   38
LAWRENCE A. ENGLANDER

5. Beyond Autonomy and Authority:
The New Dilemma of Liberal Judaism   53
MICHAEL L. MORGAN

6. Mitzvah and Autonomy   65
HERBERT BRONSTEIN

7. Mending the World and the Evil Inclination:
The Human Role in Redemption   83
MICHAEL S. STROH

◌ II : Mitzvah in Our Lives

8. Brushes with the Sacred:
An Experiential Approach to Mitzvah   95
NILES E. GOLDSTEIN

9. The Four Questions of Reform Jewish Life   108
ELYSE GOLDSTEIN

10. A Voice in the Dark: How Do We Hear God?   115
ELYSE D. FRISHMAN

◌ Part III : Doing Mitzvot

11. Re-creating the Narrative Community,
or It's Hard to Do Mitzvot by Yourself   129
PETER S. KNOBEL

12. The Command to Study   142
ANDREW N. BACHMAN

13. Leviat ha-Met: Honoring Our Dead   153
SUE LEVI ELWELL

Notes on Contributors   165

Introduction

By nearly every statistical criterion—educational level, economic status, professional position—Jews are one of the most successful groups in America today. Yet the Jewish leadership is in crisis. As we face the next century, Jews seem to have become victims of their own success. Despite their power and affluence within American society, the future of Jewish practice and culture is in serious doubt. The rites, rituals, and ceremonies that for centuries have animated our religious lives are now largely ignored. Many are not even aware of some of our most beautiful and moving traditions.

But times are changing. A growing self-awareness about our problems has sparked a spiritual renaissance. Across the denominational spectrum Jews are striving to learn more about their heritage. Adult education classes are on the rise throughout the country. More and more parents are enrolling their children in Jewish day schools. On the grassroots level, old rituals are being rediscovered and observed. The kosher food industry is in a period of tremendous growth. Some synagogues are drawing overflow crowds at Friday night services. People are yearning for more than what secular American culture can provide.

Despite its historical ambivalence toward religious ritual, the Reform movement is also part of this shift. In addition to the retrieval of Jewish behaviors and symbols that were once discarded (such as the wearing of head coverings and prayer shawls during worship), some Reform Jews are beginning to create new ones. As Reform rabbis, we are writing this book to add our voices to this resurgence of Jewish life and creativity. The liberal movements have always stood at the cutting edge of religious thought. Sometimes they have offered visions of the future. Sometimes they have simply cut away at the past. The question now is: *What happens next?*

One of the core principles in the Jewish tradition is that of mitzvah, variously translated as good deed, sanctum, or commandment. What all the writers in this book share is a commitment to the centrality of mitzvah (mitzvot in its plural form and its real-life applications) and to the belief that mitzvah will be the key to Jewish continuity, the basis for its spiritual renewal. What exactly are mitzvot? Are they things that can change with time and place? If mitzvot are not the literal expression of God's will, then what is the source of their authority and power? Why should modern Jews take them seriously? Can we create new mitzvot? If so, are there any guidelines to help us or boundaries that govern us? These are just some of the questions our essays will seek to address.

Though the Reform movement has been grappling with the ideas of commandments and commandedness in different ways for a number of years, this book is largely the result of discussions between members of a small group of rabbis called the Reform Roundtable. In the spring of 1996, this group held a two-day meeting in Toronto devoted solely to issues of liberal Jewish theology and observance. Its purpose, at the brink of the next century, was to begin thinking of ways through which to create a more "religious" Reform Judaism, a movement whose hallmark would be not only the pursuit of social justice (as has often been the case for over a century) but also its sacred relationship to God through worship and ritual observance.

Duties of the Soul is a collection of essays, and it reflects the views of its individual authors. The three sections of the book offer a program for the contemporary liberal Jew. All the essays, reflect a dissatisfaction with the status quo. Liberal Judaism is at the end of an era, but the outlines of its new forms are only beginning to emerge. All the authors share a sense that unlimited autonomy, as individual idiosyncratic choice, is not authentically Jewish nor likely to sustain a viable Judaism. Yet the authors are wary of any solution that merely advocates a return to traditional practice and belief without also calling for reinterpretation and creativity.

Part One of the book tries to identify the core issues and offers a theological and intellectual framework to address them. Daniel Bronstein provides a historical overview of Reform Judaism's relationship with mitzvah, an ambivalent relationship that has stimulated both soul-searching and creative development within the movement. Arnold Jacob Wolf writes that Judaism and mitzvot are analogous terms, that the mitzvot are simply our response to God's teaching and God's love. Our task, he writes, is to "ritualize the ethical" and "ethicize the ritual." Eric H. Yoffie argues that mitzvah must be treated as the organizing principle of Reform Judaism, the concretization of ethics and theology into daily living. Although liberal Jews are free to choose how to observe their Judaism, they should aspire to feel "commanded" by mitzvot. Lawrence Englander provides a mystical paradigm for mitzvah, arguing that we must not only strive to recover many halachic traditions but also to discover traditions that have been "lost" in our fractured world. Michael Morgan and Herbert Bronstein compare the ideas of classical authority and personal autonomy as they relate to mitzvot. Morgan claims that our new era requires new language and new categories for discussing religious observance. Bronstein argues that modern Jews have prized—to our religious detriment—personal autonomy over divine authority and that postmodern Jews must begin to rethink that balance. Michael Stroh thinks that *geulah* (redemption) is a primary Jewish category and the goal of the rabbinic system, and asks, What are the comparative roles of God and humanity in this task? If Reform Judaism reassesses its views of human nature and divine power, what impact might this have on its long-held commitment to social action?

In Part Two, we will look at the spiritual journeys of those who are addressing some of these questions, not through theory but through reflection on their own experiences. This narrative approach also invites readers to identify with and compare their own journeys to those of the authors. Whether through biblical narrative, *aggadah,* or *midrash*, listening to the stories of others teaches us how to live. Using examples from his own spiritual journey, Niles Goldstein presents an experiential approach to mitzvah, claiming that in postmodern times only the promise of the direct and immediate experience of the holy can serve as a motivation for religious behavior. For mitzvot to remain alive for us today, they must be viewed and felt as catalysts for spiritual encounter. Elyse Goldstein focuses on the paradoxes of living within a movement philosophically but on its fringes in terms of her level of ritual practice. As liberal Jews we must learn to *"drash"* (creatively interpret) every mitzvah while still longing for the *"pshat"* (simple explanation) of its truth. Elyse Frishman suggests that our interpretation of God's voice in the Bible might be linked to gender and other issues, that how we *hear* God is not necessarily identical to what God actually wants of us. In her view, the survival of Judaism and Jewish life depends less on the notion of commandedness than on our ongoing religious creativity.

In Part Three, we confront the fact that it is only through action, through *doing*, that we ultimately discover the meaning of mitzvah. As it is written in the Talmud, "Would that My people abandon Me and keep My Torah, for then they would find Me." This section of the book examines the practical side of mitzvah. Peter Knobel writes that the recovery of mitzvah requires the rebuilding of observant narrative communities—groups of praying, studying, and practicing Jews who identify the Jewish story as their own. If mitzvot are the reenactment of the Jewish people's encounter with God at Sinai, one response is to create subgroups within congregations that establish "minicovenants" around mitzvot. Andrew Bachman explores the classic Jewish notion of *talmud torah lishmah*, the study of Torah as an end in itself. Using the examples of the early Mussar movement, he advocates a new Reform agenda that makes Torah study a new and indispensable modern mitzvah. Sue Levi Elwell claims that the mitzvah of *leviat ha-met*, the accompanying of the dead, is one of the most powerful and healing rites in Judaism but that many of its attendant ritual practices are virtually unknown in liberal Jewish circles. She describes how several modern communities have reclaimed this vital mitzvah and offers new blessings and chants for its practice.

◌ ◌

The editors would like to express our gratitude to the UAHC Press for its faith in this project, as well as for the professionalism of its staff. We thank Seymour Rossel and Bennett Lovett-Graff, who commissioned this book. We are grateful to Stuart Benick, Hara Person, and Annette Abramson, who are a pleasure to work with and who are taking Reform publications into areas that are timely and important to the future of our movement. We would like especially to thank Bonny Fetterman, whose extensive experience and strict attention to detail have been invaluable to us as authors. We would also like to thank our respective religious communities, the Jewish Life Network in New York City and Beth Emet the Free Synagogue in Evanston, Illinois, for serving as sounding boards for many of these ideas.

Before performing a mitzvah, Jews say: *Baruch Atah Adonai, Eloheinu Melech ha-olam, asher kidshanu b'mitzvotav, v'tzivanu* . . . . "We praise You, Eternal God, Ruler of the universe, who sanctifies us with Your commandments, and who has commanded us to . . ."

May every reader of this book find the proper words with which to conclude the blessing.

NILES E. GOLDSTEIN
PETER S. KNOBEL

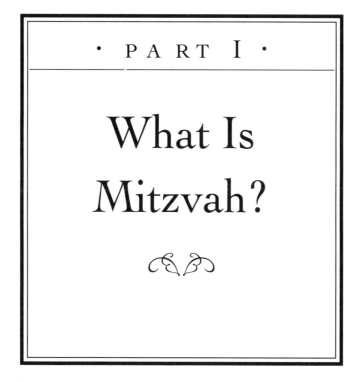

· PART I ·

What Is
Mitzvah?

Reform Judaism and Mitzvot:
A Historical Overview[1]

DANIEL M. BRONSTEIN

The North American Context

Since the onset of modern Jewish life, Jews have grappled with the basic question of who should decide how to observe Judaism: traditional rabbinical authorities, the individual, or the "community"? As late as 1844, the early American Jewish spiritual leader Isaac Leeser wrote that Jews "have no ecclesiastical authorities in America other than the congregations themselves. Each congregation makes its own rules for its government and elects its own minister, who is appointed without any ordination, induction in office being made through his election."[2] Sixty years later, Rabbi Jacob Joseph, chosen as the "chief rabbi" of New York's "downtown Jews," died, a "broken man from years of struggle to bring order to immigrant Jewish religious life."[3] "Life in Europe was geared to meet the needs and requirements of Judaism," explains historian Aaron Rothkoff. "Rabbis, scholars, and sextons were ever present to guide the faithful Jewish masses. In turn of

---

1: This essay relies heavily upon Michael A. Meyer's *Response to Modernity: A History of the Reform Movement in Judaism* (New York: Oxford University Press, 1990). Portions of this essay have also been taken from Daniel M. Bronstein, "From Denominationalism to Sectarianism: The Rise and Fall of the Synagogue Council of America" (rabbinic thesis, HUC-JIR, 1996).

2: See Leon A. Jick, *The Americanization of the Synagogue: 1820–1870* (Hanover, NH: Brandeis University Press, 1992), 68.

3: See Jeffrey S. Gurock, "Resisters and Accommodators: Varieties of Orthodox Rabbis in America, 1886–1983," in Jacob Rader Marcus and Abraham J. Peck, eds., *The American Rabbinate: A Century of Continuity and Change 1883–1983* (Hoboken: Ktav, 1985), 20.

the century America, however, the new arrival was immediately caught up in a strange world where he no longer could consult the rabbis and scholars he knew so well back home."[4] If Orthodox rabbinical authority was balkanized in New York City, then the state of traditional authority was no less than anarchic on a national level. The difficulties faced by Leeser and Joseph alike—despite vast differences in background, outlook, and historical context—still point to the same realities of North American Jewish life.

Judaism thrived in the freedom of the New World even while this very freedom persistently conflicted with traditional Jewish modalities of authority and the observance of mitzvot. While pre-Enlightenment Jewish communities were corporate in structure, Jewish life in America was grounded in the spirit of individualism. Although Jews in the "old country" were religiously guided and governed by recognized religious authorities, the Jews of America lived in an atmosphere of religious, political, and economic freedom. Both Leeser and Joseph faced the problem of establishing Jewish religious authority within a decentralized Jewish community spread over a vast continent. Jokes abound about putting two Jews in a room and getting three opinions; however, the realities of North American Jewish life presented unforeseen difficulties for traditional Judaism. Rabbi Eliezer Silver of Agudas Yisrael, a longtime leader of twentieth-century Orthodoxy, used to maintain that he was the Chief Rabbi of the United States and "Canada," (as he liked to add). However, there has never been an authoritative Chief Rabbi or rabbinate for the entirety of North American Jewry. In practical terms, this means that there has never been a North American rabbinical authority empowered to direct North American Jewry in the observance of mitzvot.

Colonial American Jews rapidly evolved from being what historian Jonathan Sarna has termed a "synagogue community" into a "community of synagogues."[5] Judaism in North America lacked a central authority for several reasons. First, the separation of church and state was legally enshrined in the United States. In the absence of a state church mandating particular beliefs and practices—as was the case throughout

---

4: Aaron Rothkoff, *Bernard Revel: Builder of American Jewish Orthodoxy* (Philadelphia: Jewish Publication Society of America, 1972), 3.

5: See Jonathan D. Sarna, "Evolution of the American Synagogue," in Norman J. Cohen and Robert M. Seltzer, eds., *The Americanization of the Jews* (New York: New York University Press, 1995), 215–29.

Europe—religious expression thrived and multiplied in the New World. In fact, the landscape of American religion is so pluralistic that Martin E. Marty, a scholar of American religion, has characterized it as "bewildering."[6]

Likewise, American religion is founded upon the system of voluntarism, meaning that since there is no centralized state church compelling affiliation and a particular religious practice, an individual's religious affiliation (or lack thereof) is made on a voluntary basis. Implicitly, since denominations lack the coercive authority to establish and enforce membership, they must compete with one another in recruiting and maintaining members. Stated in a more vulgar fashion, religious denominations mirror the world of business inasmuch as they must "sell" one particular religious system over another. Given this reality, voluntarism has compelled religious denominations, including the various streams of American Judaism, to base their systems of religious guidance upon the needs and desires of laypeople rather than solely follow the traditional halachic framework.

Indeed, American Judaism began as a layperson-led operation and lacked a trained rabbinate willing to guide its flock until well into the nineteenth century. The very creation of an American rabbinate coincided, not so coincidentally, with the further division of North American Jewry along denominational lines. However, even a denominationalized Judaism did not insure a centralized authority within the different streams of Judaism, whether Reform, Conservative, Reconstructionist, or Orthodox. In fact, each denomination of Judaism is as much a coalition as a "movement," and North American Orthodoxy—seemingly the most unified religious group— also lacks a central authority.[7] Finally, the ideological faultlines among Jews are further exacerbated by intra-Jewish ethnic differences as well as differences in geography and socioeconomic status. But the lack of authority was not always problematic for North American Jews or for Reform Jews in particular.

6: Martin E. Marty, *A Nation of Behavers*, (Chicago: University of Chicago Press, 1976), 18.

7: The term *Orthodoxy* is itself a misnomer, given that Orthodox Judaism encompasses a vast spectrum of practice and belief, ranging from what Jeffrey Gurock has explained as those "accommodating" to American cultural realities to those who "resist" these realities.

The Origins of American Reform Judaism

Decades before Reform Judaism blossomed in the New World, Jews were innovating, changing, and Americanizing Jewish practice, outside of traditional communal structures regulating the mitzvah system. Jacksonian-era Jews translated their prayers into English, listened to their spiritual leaders preach their sermons in English, and edited the liturgy.[8] Following the lead of the Reform Congregation of Berlin in 1845, the innovation of mixed-sex seating at New York's Temple Emanu-El in 1854 attracted far less attention than might have been expected, considering that "separate seating of one form or another characterized Jewish worship from early medieval times onward."[9] Rather than engaging in a halachic process or confronting the palpable clash between mitzvot and contemporaneous culture, North American Jews of the eighteenth and the first half of the nineteenth century were driven to innovation and change by practical considerations, such as a desire for a greater sense of "decorum" in their houses of worship. Moreover, the proto-Reform Jews of the New World differed from their Central European counterparts in certain respects. "In Germany," Leon Jick explains,"reform was viewed as the precursor to acculturation and integration. In America, acculturation and integration proved to be the precursors of reform."[10]

However, any discussion of contemporary Reform Judaism must also acknowledge that there was never a monolithic Reform movement in North America, in regard to either practice or theology. Today, varieties of Reform Judaism coexist, including "classical" Reform and the Reform Judaism of summer camps. One way of viewing Reform Judaism is to distinguish between the classical era—the period preceding the Columbus Platform—and the period following it. The classical period lasting roughly from the 1880s through the 1930s was perhaps

---

8: See Jick, *The Americanization of the Synagogue*; and for a documentary record of the Americanization process, see Salo W. Baron and Joseph L. Blau, eds., *The Jews of the United States, 1790–1840: A Documentary History*, 3 vols. (New York: Columbia University Press, 1963), and Jacob Rader Marcus, ed., *The Jew in the American World: A Source Book* (Detroit: Wayne State University Press, 1996).

9: See Jonathan D. Sarna, "The Debate over Mixed Seating in the American Synagogue," in Jack Wertheimer, ed., *The American Synagogue: A Sanctuary Transformed* (New York: Cambridge University Press, 1987), 364, 368.

10: Jick, *The Americanization of the Synagogue*, 80.

the time of greatest cohesiveness both in terms of ideological integrity and in regard to questions of authority and mitzvah. In fact, the existence of a halachic, mitzvah-based system of Judaism engendered neither concern nor a sense of obligation for Reform leaders in the classical period. Classical Reform spoke not in terms of "mitzvah" but rather used the language of the "mission of Israel." Concerning itself in the broad, modern issues of ethics and social justice, the traditional modes of observance were seen as passé. The performance of mitzvot and the traditional authority system of Judaism were rejected in accordance with the radical Reform ideology of the era. This is not to say that classical Reform Judaism, its practitioners and rabbinical leaders, were assimilationists. To the contrary, classical reformers passionately fought against assimilation in maintaining their separate Jewish identity and through their insistence that the Jewish religion, rather than ethnicity, was at the heart of Jewish identity. But Isaac Mayer Wise, the founder of Reform Judaism in America, had initially hoped to establish a new American Judaism for all New World Jews and had likewise opposed the classical or "radical" reforms of the other founding fathers of Reform Judaism. On several occasions he attempted to establish a central communal organization for American Jews, and he hoped to bind Jews together with his prayer book, *Minhag America*. Wise did his utmost to create a centralized system of American Judaism enshrining very specific guidelines regarding mitzvot and theology.

From 1841 through 1855, both Wise and Leeser attempted to organize American Jews through a common liturgy, religious organization, and system for Jewish education. Wise was prepared to forgo various elements of the emerging radical Reform ideology. Hoping to maintain the semblance of unity binding the religiously disparate community of American Jews, Wise's dreams were rapidly overturned by the growing and bewildering reality of Jewish denominationalism in America. But he nonetheless attempted to overcome the divisions of American Jewry.

Backed by the laity's demand for intra-Jewish unity, he attempted to realize this dream through the establishment of the Union of American Hebrew Congregations (UAHC) and the Hebrew Union College (HUC). Aspiring toward a unified American rabbinical seminary, Wise believed that HUC would produce spiritual leaders capable of serving the entirety of American Jewry. Likewise, as Michael A. Meyer points out, the "propagation of Reform Judaism was neither an overt nor a covert purpose of the UAHC. Not only would the discussion of doctrinal and ritual issues have threatened to break up the still fragile union, but it appeared that with greater or lesser rapidity nearly all of American Jewry was in any case moving at least toward moderate Reform."[11] However, when the disparate segments of the Union gathered for the first annual ordination of HUC students in 1883—at the "high[est] point of Jewish religious unity in America"—the laypeople responsible for catering the event "carelessly ordered" a dinner featuring a "variety of shellfish," and this short-lived period of American Jewish unity was inevitably torn asunder by ritual disagreements.[12]

The scandalous "Terefah Banquet" was symbolic of the vast differences separating American Jews in regard to the mitzvah system. In other words, conflicts over religious authority and the mitzvah system had reemerged. After attempting to sweep religious differences under the rug, American Jews learned that the desire for religious freedom was stronger than the dream of unity. Thus, in the course of the nineteenth century, the radical wing of the Reform movement triumphed and its views persisted as a living ideology well into the next century. As Michael Meyers writes, "The last decades of the nineteenth century and the first years of the twentieth witnessed the widest swing of the Reform pendulum away from traditional Jewish belief and practice . . . as it distinguished itself more sharply from Orthodoxy and from an emergent Conservative Judaism." These distinctions served to strengthen the process of denominationalization.[13]

Classical Reform Judaism

The swing of the pendulum was most clearly articulated in the Central Conference of American Rabbis' (CCAR) 1885 declaration known as the Pittsburgh Platform. This statement sought to distinguish Reform ideology both from "wholly nonsectarian universal" and from the "more traditional expressions of Judaism."[14] Rabbi Emil G. Hirsch, a preeminent leader of classical Reform, declared that the Reform mis-

---

11: Meyer, *Response to Modernity,* 262.
12: Ibid., 263.
13: Ibid., 264.
14: Ibid., 265.

sion was to "participate in the great task of modern times, to solve on the basis of justice and righteousness the problems presented by the contrasts and evils of the present organization of society."[15] The Reformers' clear emphasis on social justice and the relegation of traditional ritual and practice to secondary importance accelerated the process of the denominationalization of American Judaism.

"[T]oday we accept as binding only the moral laws, and maintain only such ceremonies as elevate and sanctify our lives," the 1885 statement read, "but reject all such as are not adapted to the views and habits of modern civilization."[16] Distinguishing between those religious observances deemed relevant and those considered irrelevant to the modern world might have allowed for some openness toward mitzvot and the mitzvah system. The authors of the Pittsburgh Platform also insisted however that "all such Mosaic and rabbinical laws as regulate diet, priestly purity, and dress . . . fail to impress the modern Jew" and that their "observance in our days is apt rather to obstruct than to further modern spiritual elevation." This was not simply a rejection of particular mitzvot, but a clear nullification of the very concept of the mitzvah system.

By the turn of the century, the Hebrew Union College, modeled after theologically liberal Protestant seminaries and relying upon modern scholarly methods, was institutionally opposed to consideration of a return to the mitzvah system. HUC president Kaufmann Kohler forbade the wearing of *kipot* and *tallitot*.[17] "Not by Romanticism or Ritualism or Legalism," Kohler stated in 1904, "but by the accentuation of the eternal principles of our eternal truths can our faith be revitalized."[18]

Even so, by the 1920s Reform Judaism was challenged by changing demographic realities. The absorption of Eastern European Jews into the Reform movement altered attitudes among Reform leaders and laypeople. By the second decade of the century, the Reform rabbinate included many Eastern Europeans in its ranks, who, along with rabbis of German descent, began to tear down classical Reform's opposition to Zionism.[19] More significantly, on the religious level, Reform began its

---

15: Ibid.

16: Quoted from Meyer, *Response to Modernity*, 388.

17: See Howard M. Sachar, *A History of Jews in America* (New York: Alfred A. Knopf, 1992), 390–91.

18: Ibid., 390.

slow return to the more traditional rituals of Shabbat and High Holy Day observance—such as the *Kol Nidre* service—and facilitated the "restoration" of such holidays as Purim and Chanukah.[20] As secular Jewish organizations, such as B'nai B'rith, continued to grow in influence, the "persistent question addressed by rabbis and laity in this period was therefore how to stem the synagogue's continuing drift toward the periphery" of Jewish life.[21] Given the new openness to some traditional mitzvot, Reform Jews began to question whether the mitzvah system could still be rejected in its entirety.

As Leon Jick argues, "Perhaps even more significant than the diversification of ethnic origin" in the Reform movement was the "transformation of political and economic circumstances and the drastic alteration of expectations that came to pass in the 1930s."[22] For almost a century, modernity was viewed by Reformers as an actual and prime ideational agent for bringing about the messianic kingdom. In a broad sense, Reformers were no different in this respect from Conservatives, modern Orthodox, not to mention modern Christians, or a great variety of non-Western peoples. The West had, after all, ostensibly emerged from a long and dark age. Over the entire globe, the West was on the move, working through technology and culture, economics and Christianity, to enlighten all non-Westerners, including Jews, to Western civilization. Reformers pointed to the twinned events of Emancipation and Enlightenment, allowing for their economic, cultural, and, to an extent, social entry into the "real" civilization. It appeared that a new era of universal brotherhood was just around the corner, and this modernized idea of the kingdom of God would come about through all the modern tools of technology, culture, and politics, all of which was grounded in the faith in reason rather than in a commitment to the tradition.

Yet, by the 1930s the entire world had been torn asunder by global economic depression, the rise of fascism and Stalinism, and the rise of Nazism in the heart of Western civilization. The tumultuous events of the 1930s brought into question previously positive assessments about modernity and the West in general. Even American Jews, sheltered as

---

19: Ibid., 100.

20: Ibid.

21: Meyer, *Response to Modernity*, 303–4.

22: See Leon A. Jick, "The Reform Synagogue," in Wertheimer, ed., *The American Synagogue*, 99.

they were from events in Europe, experienced perhaps the most rabid, native anti-Semitism in the nation's history. This development added to the sense of being unwelcome in the wake of the enactment of anti-Semitic legislation in 1924 regarding immigration quotas. But if the promises of modernity had been fleeting, Judaism had proven itself quite resilient through centuries of history. If modernity was being reappraised, so too was the tradition.

The Reassessment of Tradition: The Columbus Platform

Judging from UAHC surveys taken in 1928 and 1930, traditional rituals "at least for the leadership . . . were assuming much greater importance than in the classical past."[23] Likewise, by 1938, a joint committee of the UAHC and the CCAR on "Ceremonies" was established in order to revive and create new rituals. On a parallel track, the UAHC published guides for practice, and in the mid-1940s Rabbi Solomon Freehof began his "decades-long endeavor to link actual Reform practice through traditional customs" with his groundbreaking work to establish Reform responsa.[24] In returning to the use of the traditional form and methodology of responsa literature, Freehof sought at the very least to change Reform practice by transforming the methods in which Reform Jews determined their religious practices. "Judaism is a religion that was formed by law and has lived by law," Freehof argued, and it was clear to him that "Reform Judaism must come to an understanding with the law or at least must define clearly its own relationship to it."[25] This movement toward reappraisal was most fully expressed through the 1935 CCAR declaration known as the Columbus Platform.

In a radical reversal, the Reform rabbinate began its return to a more traditional sense of thinking and to traditional categories of Judaism— God, Torah, and Israel.[26] Rather than entirely dismissing the traditional conceptions toward law and observance, the Columbus Platform states that the "Torah, both written and oral, enshrines Israel's ever-growing

---

23: Meyer, *Response to Modernity*, 322.

24: Ibid., 322–25.

25: Solomon B. Freehof, "Reform Judaism and the Halacha," in Joseph L. Blau, ed., *Reform Judaism: A Historical Perspective* (New York: Ktav, 1973), 322.

26: Meyer, *Response to Modernity*, 319.

consciousness of God and of the moral law. It preserves the historical precedents, sanctions, and norms of Jewish life and seeks to mould it in the patterns of goodness and holiness." More to the point, some "laws have lost their binding force with the passing of the conditions"; every "age has the obligation to adapt the teachings of the Torah to its basic needs in consonance with the genius of Judaism."[27] Thus, while propagating neither a full return to traditional Judaism nor unconditional adherence to a mitzvah system, the 1935 declaration showed a far greater appreciation of the enduring value of the tradition as well as greater openness to the observance of mitzvot. Moreover, the platform referred to the desirability of an authoritative Reform framework for religious observance. "Judaism as a way of life," wrote the authors, "requires in addition to its moral and spiritual demands, the preservation of the Sabbath, festivals, and Holy Days, the retention and development of such customs, symbols, and ceremonies as possess inspirational value." In other words, the Columbus statement argued that certain religious standards and practices were necessary for one to live an integral Jewish life.

Reform Judaism after World War II

Tensions within Reform theology, practices, and the ideal of *klal Yisrael* became a far greater concern for the Reform rabbinate after the Holocaust. *Klal Yisrael,* the concept of Jewish peoplehood—inclusive of all Jews, regardless of nationality, religious outlook, or ideology—became an important aspect of Reform Judaism. More than ever, Reform Jews conceived of themselves as being part of a larger people. As historian Salo Baron explained, it had become clear in the postwar years that "religion was not altogether the 'private affair of the individual,' which many liberals and Socialists had long thought it to be."[28]

The need for greater self-definition of Reform practice and belief in this period paralleled the drive toward greater unity within the movement. In the 1950s, an increasing number of Reform rabbis attempted to create a theological framework for religious practice, leading to the

---

27: Ibid., 389.
28: See Salo W. Baron, *Steeled by Adversity: Essays and Addresses on American Jewish Life* (Philadelphia: Jewish Publication Society of America,1971), 419.

publication of a series of guidebooks explicating religious practices for Reform Jews.[29] One such manual, *Reform Judaism: A Guide for Reform Jews,* was written by Rabbi Abraham J. Feldman of Hartford, Connecticut, in 1953.[30] Based in part on the Columbus Platform, Feldman's guidebook was also designed to distinguish Reform from Orthodox Judaism.[31] For example, in the section titled *"Tallis,"* Feldman wrote that it is "not customary in Reform synagogues to wear the *tallis* or prayer shawl. The Tallis is an oriental garb coming from a time when people going to formal functions would wear this outer garment. It served the same function as did in New England communities the 'Sunday-go-to-meetin' clothes.' When our people were exiled from Judea to Western lands, and the outer cloak was no longer the form of garb worn on formal occasions, there was no reason for perpetuating it in the form of a prayer shawl. Hence, Reform discontinued the use of the *tallis,* even as in Orthodox and Conservative synagogues the *tallis* has shrunk to a proportion of a mere scarf."[32] But while Feldman may have maintained a more "classical" position in this instance, the tensions between ideological integrity, the reappropriation of some mitzvot, and the hope for greater religious unity among American Jews can be documented throughout the 1950s.

At the June 1951 convention of the CCAR, Conservative and Reform rabbis discussed a proposed merger between Reform and Conservative Judaism but ultimately dismissed it because of ongoing ideological and ritual differences. Despite the expressed interest within the leadership of the Reform rabbinate for greater unity, the practical consideration of ideological autonomy transcended the ideal of unity or an authoritative position on the mitzvah system. This ambivalence was expressed at the CCAR convention of 1954, as participants sounded a less than certain note on the efficacy of Reform Judaism as the exclusive form of American Judaism. Addressing the questions surrounding the future of Reform Judaism, Rabbi James G. Heller, a prominent Reform rabbi, stated that "by correlating ourselves with our time and also our desire to remain close to *klal Yisrael,* by endless concern over the

---

29: Meyer, *Response to Modernity,* 376.

30: Abraham J. Feldman, *Reform Judaism: A Guide for Reform Jews* (Hartford, CT: Temple Beth Israel, 1953).

31: Ibid., 5–6.

32: Ibid.

balancing of authority and freedom: only thus can we justify our claims to be the exponents of a living marching Judaism."[33]

In the mid-1950s the CCAR remained conflicted in its quest for unity and its own ideological and theological self-preservation. By this time, three trends had become defined within the leadership of the Reform rabbinate. There were those such as CCAR president Joseph Fink, who felt that Reform occupied the ideological center, attacked both by a stubbornly segregationist Orthodox rabbinate and by the Reform-populated anti-Zionist organization, the American Council for Judaism, which then threatened to splinter the Reform movement. Others, such as Feldman, still believed that Reform Judaism would become synonymous with American Judaism. He felt that the Reform movement needed further definition while continuing to stake out its proper ideological position between an archaic traditionalism on one side and vague moral and religious anarchy on the other. Finally, there were those like Heller, who explicitly questioned long-held classical Reform ideological tenets and stressed closer cooperation with Conservative Judaism while leaving open the future possibility of the unification of non-Orthodox American Jewry.[34]

Within the context of a discussion at the 1955 CCAR convention, "Developments in Reform Judaism," the inherent conflict of the Reform movement's ideological emphasis on "reason and rationality" versus "chaos" and the "present anarchistic individualism" became a hotly debated issue.[35] Also, a drive persisted for publishing a formal "Guide of Practice" for Reform Jews.[36] In later years, Feldman played an important role in formulating a movement-wide guidebook, although he argued that the text should forgo the use of words such as "required" and "forbidden." Clearly, Feldman was seeking to preserve individual religious autonomy for Reform Jews. Nevertheless, he agreed that "Reform Judaism has developed through the years a unique character and a recognizable pattern of observance, and that these ought to be made known to our congregants by means of an unofficial guide."[37] In fact, Meyer reports that, by 1953, 85 percent of Reform Jews "favored a

---

33: 1954 CCAR Yearbook, 167.

34: Leon Jick writes that, by this time, distinctions between Reform and Conservative synagogues had "virtually disappeared." See his essay "The Reform Synagogue," in Wertheimer, ed., *The American Synagogue*, 103.

35: *1955 CCAR Yearbook*, 178–96.

36: Ibid., 124.

37: Ibid., 126.

guide to help them select practices voluntarily" but that only "about a third of the laypeople and 28 percent of the rabbis were ready to accept an authoritative code."[38] Also by the 1950s, other Reform rabbis began to produce their own guides for Reform practice, although the tensions remained between setting a standard practice of mitzvot on the one hand and making mitzvot obligatory on the other. The most important effort was *A Guide for Reform Jews,* by Rabbis Frederic A. Doppelt and David Polish, in 1957. While "speaking in the language of mitzvot," it remained ideologically Reform by virtue of the "authors' readiness not only to dispense with many of the traditional mitzvot, especially the prohibitions, but boldly to introduce new ones."[39]

Nevertheless, alongside the benefits of clearly delineated religious practice and observance for Reform Judaism, an authoritative set of specific guidelines carried a number of potential risks. First, how could a movement based upon both reason and an autonomous response to religious needs ideologically reconcile itself to an authoritative guide? Moreover, some Reform Jews still believed in certain ritual standards and were unwilling to forgo some of the fundamental traditions of Judaism.

For example, in 1955 the president of the CCAR, Rabbi Barnett Brickner, supported the ordination of women by urging a "break with tradition." He was influenced by developments within American Protestantism, as well as debate on this subject within the Conservative movement's Rabbinical Assembly of America (RAA).[40] Nonetheless, Brickner confronted what the *New York Times* called "vigorous opposition" from those rabbis who believed that "the ordination of women would constitute a 'decisive' schism within American Judaism."[41] Rabbi Solomon B. Freehof, the major formulator of Reform religious practices, counseled caution before "brushing aside two thousand years of Jewish practice."[42] Ultimately, the CCAR decided to postpone a resolution of the issue in the interest of further study.[43]

In his 1955 presidential address, Brickner spoke about the conflict between autonomy and authority, which impacted upon Reform Ju-

---

38 Meyer, *Response to Modernity,* 376.

39: Ibid.

40:*New York Times,* June 21, 1955.

41: Ibid., June 22,1955.

42: Ibid., June 24,1955.

43: Ibid.

daism's relationship with the other streams of American Judaism. "What," he asked, " are the minimum standards for being a Reform Jew?"[44] Despite vast differences in religious practice and observance among American Jews, Brickner maintained that "since the Jewish community of America is becoming more homogeneous and stabilized . . . we must continue a process which the founding fathers of Reform invented; that is, shaping Judaism for the Western world into a living faith."[45]

Ultimately, the rabbinic leadership of the Reform movement in the mid-1950s was unable to formulate a precise and authoritative religious code for all Reform Jews. Since the Reform rabbinate itself was unable to devise a unified ideological stand, it could hardly propose and advocate a universal standard of mitzvot.

Contemporary Reform Judaism: The Conflict between Mitzvah and Autonomy

By the 1970s, the CCAR had published guides for Shabbat observance and life-cycle ritual, yet they remained "theologically vague, reserving interpretation of the word 'mitzvah' to four divergent appended essays." These "books did provide evidence that Reform Judaism possessed standards of practice, even though they represented an ideal."[46]

This ambivalence was also reflected in the San Francisco Platform, or Centenary Perspective, of 1976, which came to fruition under Eugene B. Borowitz, the preeminent theologian of Reform Judaism. The Centenary Perspective maintained that Reform Judaism shared the traditional "emphasis on duty and obligation."[47] However, even while noting that Reform Jews were obliged to study, worship, and observe Judaism on a daily basis, as well as keep the Sabbath and holy days, the Centenary statement also maintained that within "each area of Jewish observance Reform Jews are called upon to confront the claims of Jewish tradition, however differently perceived, and to exercise their individual autonomy, choosing and creating on the basis of commitment

---

44: *1955 CCAR Yearbook,* 12.
45: Ibid., 11.
46: Meyer, *Response to Modernity,* 377.
47: Ibid., 393.

and knowledge." Reflective of the larger postwar trend in Reform Judaism, the Centenary Perspective demonstrated a continued desire to reintegrate the tradition into Reform Jewish life. But although Reform practice was reinvigorated with some traditional rituals and liturgy, a basic philosophical problem remained: How could personal autonomy coexist with a mitzvah system? Thus, even while attempting to place mitzvah as an essential aspect of Reform Judaism, Reform Jews remained ambivalent about creating a centralized mitzvah system obligating specific religious practices.

In recent years, notable efforts have been made by Rabbi Walter Jacob, with the establishment of the Freehof Institute of Progressive Halakhah. Jacob and others have continued to struggle with the theological and practical problems in creating a Reform mitzvah system. Rather than speaking in terms of custom, as Freehof had, these efforts attempted to fashion a conceptual basis for the observance of mitzvot. As Jacob and Moshe Zemer argued, A Reform or "progressive" system of *halachah* must "give priority to ethical dimensions in applying *mitzvot* to life . . . view *kedushah* (holiness) as a rationale for evaluating commandments, and . . . provide some role to the individual conscience in determining halachic choice."[48] Nevertheless, the conflicting desire for individual autonomy, on the one hand, and an authoritative Reform mitzvah system, on the other, persists into the present.[49]

Conclusions

Jacob Rader Marcus, the late dean of American Jewish history, wrote:

> All through the nineteenth and early twentieth century there were men who believed that one central national body would be good for the Jews; it would bring them security, strength. Ethnicity would cement them all. This centripetal drive, however, was halted by factors that were apparently contradictory. Jews were

---

48: Walter Jacob and Moshe Zemer, "Introduction," in Jacob and Zemer, eds., *Dynamic Jewish Law: Progressive Halakhah, Essence and Application* (Pittsburgh: Rodef Shalom Press, 1991), 5.

49: See also Walter Jacob, ed., *Liberal Judaism and Halakhah* (Pittsburgh: Rodef Shalom Press, 1988).

particularistic; they were kept apart by different ideologies; Orthodoxy, Reform, socialism were at war with one another; loyalties were parochial, limited to congregations and hometown societies. Yet there was at the same time a strong desire on the part of most immigrants to become an integral part of the American totality. This tension between particularism and regionalism, and Americanism did not tear Jews apart; the American pull always won out as long as one's Jewish identity was not threatened.[50]

Marcus has noted the powerful pull of the majority culture in which all of us live; a culture grounded in the belief in freedom and the autonomy of the individual. But it is more than possible that the ongoing confrontation between autonomy and authority will never be fully resolved for Reform Jews. The retention of individual religious freedom is seemingly inconsistent with full participation in an authoritative, mitzvah-based system of Judaism. If we decide as a community to preserve the ceasefire between mitzvah and freedom, Reform Jews will have to persist in devising creative solutions for establishing and maintaining the sense of obligation toward mitzvot, as did our forebears. However, given our continued belief in the desirability of an authoritative mitzvah system, Reform Jews may decide to relegate the philosophy of personal autonomy to a lower rung in our belief system. This, of course, would mean that Reform Judaism would become a denomination forbidding some types of behavior while mandating other rituals, and that appears antithetical to Reform ideology. No matter how vague the future, we can still take comfort in the vibrancy of a community willing to examine itself and willing—like the authors of both the Pittsburgh and Columbus platforms—to reassess its position and consider change.

50: Jacob Rader Marcus, *United States Jewry, 1776–1985* (Detroit: Wayne State University Press, 1989), 4:566.

Back to the Future:
On Rediscovering Commandments

ARNOLD JACOB WOLF

Only something that offends us will define Judaism. The saying that defines Judaism best, and is deeply offensive to us, is: It is better to do something under command than by choice. That, I think, is the classic definition of Judaism: Mitzvah is in a privileged position, one that is deeply offensive. Because, to all of us North Americans, autonomy and choice—freedom and the ability to decide for ourselves—are crucial. But to Judaism, as I understand it, against my inclination, the opposite is the case. What is done out of choice is inferior to what is done out of command; that's my text for what follows. All of Judaism is mitzvah: There is nothing else. Rabbi Larry Kushner translates mitzvah as "response." Not a bad translation; mitzvah means more than "commandment" obviously, not less.

Reform Judaism has always affirmed mitzvot both in principle and in practice. The problem of Reform mitzvah is not the concept of mitzvah but the repertoire. In Reform Judaism, the repertoire of mitzvot was often very small. This I know from my own family. My granddaughters are fifth-generation Reform Jews (in the same congregation, by the way). Nobody in five generations of our family ever ate on Yom Kippur. Nobody in five generations ever ate bread on Pesach. Nobody in five generations ever willfully violated the ethical mitzvot, and so on. On the other hand, there were certain technical mitzvot, detailed mitzvot, that most of those generations never even heard of. Not my grandmother and not my granddaughters. They just don't know about certain elements of the repertoire, so what they might do about them is

19

hard to say; *taharat hamishpachah* (family "purity"), for example, or *sha'atnez* (clothing restrictions).

But Reform's repertoire is expanding. The most significant element of recent Reform Jewish history is the expanded number of items that are now on the agenda. Folkways or "ceremonies" for some, ritual practice for some, nationalistic expression for some, dialogic response for some; in any case, the number of items clearly is greater than it ever was in congregational life, individual Jewish lives, and community consensus. What is not clear is whether or not all this is done primarily because it is commanded. In the interpretation of lay Reform Jews, obedience is largely a matter of pick-and-choose. *We* will decide which mitzvot we accept and which ones we don't. *We* are in charge of our own religious lives.

This, I believe, is the original sin of Reform Judaism. By definition, you cannot freely choose to be commanded. An example: Eugene Borowitz wrote a fine book on sex that was, by the way, dedicated to me, a very great honor. It was called *Choosing a Sex Ethic*. His advisory editor, a well-known sociologist, Philip Rieff, said to him, "You cannot choose an ethic. The whole point of an ethic is that it comes to you. It is discovered; it is not chosen." This is a serious criticism of any notion of autonomy. Borowitz himself was always completely aware of autonomy's limits. If there is a God, there cannot be a fully autonomous human being. If there is a God, there has to be some kind of heteronomy. There has to be obedience. How you know God's will for you, and whether you're able to do God's will are difficult questions, but they are secondary to the belief that, if you know, when you know, however you know God's will, there is no choice about performing it. There is only obedience or sin.

Our task, as I see it, is to ritualize the ethical commandments and to ethicize the ritual commandments. If you understand *kashrut*, it has obvious ethical implications, ecological implications, implications for the nature of the human body, and so on. If you ritualize ethics, then you are not just a Jew who does good; you are a Jew who *has* to do good. That's why the mitzvah is always better than the person who chooses. You are not someone who sometimes, or even often, or even usually does the right thing; you are someone who is habituated—as Aristotle said we must be—to doing the right thing. You don't evaluate the possibility of not doing it. You just say "yes."

We do not constitute the obligatory; we discover it. We must recover all that we can. God has made us an offer we cannot refuse. There are some tasks we cannot ("yet," according to Franz Rosenzweig) retrieve. What we cannot retrieve should not occasion guilt. It should occasion struggle. Even God cannot expect you to do what you cannot do. The problem, of course, is that we say we cannot do X because we will not do X. That is, precisely, sin. Congregations' and movements' purpose is to assist persons and families to recover the mitzvot. Knowledge empowers, instructs, privileges, obligates, and also condemns.

What is important, I think—most important—is not the number of mitzvot performed, but the direction of our life. We are either going in or getting out. We are either recovering tradition—rediscovering Judaism was my phrase for it in the 60s—or we are abandoning it. Direction is everything. If we are in the direction—and I think we are—of recovering, then all is beginning to be better, if not yet well. If we're on our way out, then all is lost.

The other text I like, besides classical rabbinic texts, is a cartoon from the old *New Yorker*. A child in a progressive nursery school raises her hand and says, "Teacher, do we have to do what we want to do?" That's the basic question for liberal Jews. The answer is "No! You do not have to do what you want to do; you can do what you *ought* to do." The shift from want to need, from what people say they want, or even think they want, to what they really need is our crucial pedagogical task. God is only in the details. If I were truly *chutzpadik*, I would say: God *is* the details.

Most of us understand that we are obligated under God to perform a number of ethical tasks. But we do not always see these are more than just secular, humane opportunities and demands. We cannot distinguish what we do as Jews from what we do as plain, fairly good human beings. Wouldn't we help the poor or respect our parents or keep faithful in marriage even if these were not commands of the Torah?

Jewish ethics is not fully congruent with philosophic ethics or with practical reason. Jews derive our direction from texts (*Tanakh, halachah*) that are not the general property of the West. Our emphasis on this world as the arena of religious performance is not the same as Christianity's, or Marxism's for that matter. God will take care of our life in the world to come; we are responsible for bringing this world as close to the messianic ideal as possible. Holiness is not abstract or magical; it is the goal of our morality and the task of every single Jew.

The method of Jewish ethics is the case method, not theoretical deduction from first principles. Every case refers back to traditional authorities but can be decided only by what the Torah calls "a judge who will be there in your own time and situation." The process of decision making is human, since the Torah was given into our hands for interpretation. It is corrigible, since all of us are fallible. It is personal, because each of us is unique, but it always relates to community standards that are transsubjective.

Jewish ethics tries to get us to do what God wants us to do in the human world, the world of sex, of illness, of poverty, and of creativity. Judaism helps us know what God wants. A Jew can never pretend that he or she has no clue to the will of God; we are ignorant only of the nature of God. What God wants of us is called Torah and we do know what it requires. We do not, on the other hand, always know how to do what we must do, for example about divorce or vocation or politics, but we are obligated to struggle to find out.

Jews are obligated to marry each other and to raise Jewish children. We have no monastic alternative, nor do we think that the only purpose of sex is procreation. We seek *shelom bayit*, a family life that can be a matrix of ethical performance. But we also believe in the right to divorce without shame or stigma. In this we differ from many Christian Americans. On the other hand, we do not endorse whimsical or self-seeking divorce. I would think that divorce is never permitted: It is either required or forbidden (as is abortion, according to traditional Jewish law).

In this model, divorce is right only when the marriage is destructive of relationship and of personal survival. Not personal happiness. Not the desire to fulfill one's own enrichment. Not because it is too hard to make marriage work. Divorce is right only when there is literally no alternative, when two people, with the best will in the world, trying as hard as they can to help each other, find that whatever they do, the other partner is hurt. In other words, a marriage is only dissolved when it has already ended. Some of our greatest sages were divorced, though I believe none of them was proud of having been unable to sustain a valid marriage.

This example can teach us a great deal about mitzvot. If one party is brutal, abusive, or indifferent, the other has the duty, not the privilege, of ending the relationship. If there are children, their good must be considered first of all. Only if divorce is in their interest can it be justified, since divorce usually is painful and dangerous for young children, at the very least. But a failed marriage is also bad for children and must be improved or ended when improvement proves impossible.

Other examples of obligation may also be instructive. Jews are required, so far as they are able, to help other Jews. We have an obligation to support Israel, which by no means is identical with support for any given government policy there or, for that matter, a policy of the United States. We are not allowed to be bland universalists, just as we are not allowed to consider our own family the moral equivalent of all other families. Our ethical tasks begin close to home and then move in ever-widening circles until, in principle, if never in reality, we embrace the whole world. To be a Jew means to love "the near one" (neighbor) as ourselves, hoping to bring near as many as we can.

So-called ritual performance must also be endowed with ethical concern or it will be merely obsessional and idolatrous. Keeping kosher, so far as one is able, is a statement of ecological concern, respect for animal rights, and for disciplined health standards. Some of us must go beyond the prohibition of unclean animals to limit the number of calories that we ingest. The logic and lure of vegetarianism are powerful indeed. We do not agree with the New Testament passage in which Jesus says that not what goes into one's mouth but only what comes out is important. We are what we eat; the mitzvah of *kashrut* is profoundly ethical.

So are our holidays. Pesach speaks of liberation and of gratitude. It represents the freedom to be servants of God instead of serving human masters. The Days of Awe offer an opportunity to turn away from our usual self-centered concerns to the One who calls us both to regret and to redemption. *Tzedakah* is not merely charity nor even the same as the powerful Christian notion of self-sacrificing *caritas* (love). It is the disciplined (again, that word) conviction that what we have is not truly our own, but God's, as we ourselves are. Even death is an ethical opportunity to surrender not only what we have but also what we are. Death is not supposed to be easy, but it is surely inexorable.

Often we are confronted by moral contradiction and doubt. What shall we think about a Mother Teresa who loves the dying but forbids abortion even to save the life of a mother? What should we do when our country legislates for the benefit of the rich at the expense of its children and aged? What do we do when Israel invades Lebanon in an impossible hope of violently making the Galilee safe? What about medical ethics, especially, but by no means solely, end-of-life issues? Why do the latter crowd out the much more significant problems of medical insurance for every citizen and a safe environment for every child?

What shall we tell our children about premarital sex? We worry if they are active, and equally if they are not. We are not sure what we think about what they do. Should Jewish institutions (or other valid causes) accept money from tainted sources? How would we determine which gifts are unacceptable? What persons, if any, must be excluded from our community?

The system of commandments does not relieve us of choosing among religious or moral options. In fact, it often challenges us with those very choices. Even (especially) traditional Judaism was full of debate and of dissent. Liberal Jews have sometimes endorsed a liberal view of communal issues without deepening their Jewish insights. Paradoxically, without binding commandments we have often been merely simpleminded and undialectical. Judaism does not make us less responsible personally. It gives us a framework for our decisions that, as I have urged, are often difficult and for tasks that often offend our delicate sensibilities.

The origin of texts, about which we all learned in our rabbinic training, is irrelevant to the efficacy or the meaning or the validity of those texts. We were taught that if you could trace a sacred text back to human origins (easy to do), that somehow deprivileged it. If you could find out that the Torah was really written down in the seventh century B.C.E., or, as some would say, in the fifth century, and not dictated to Moses on Sinai, then somehow that made it less binding. Or if you could find that the rabbis were in certain specific ways responding to their environment's special economic and social factors, that made rabbinic law less binding. That is the genetic fallacy; origins disprove nothing. It doesn't make any difference how we got the Torah; we got it, and now it's here. We are obligated not to complete its project but also not to fail to undertake it at all.

We are all beginners, not just we Reform Jews but also all traditional Jews. We have to learn how to dance. We have the benefit not only of halachic norms but of aggadic narratives (legends, theology) and, as the poet Bialik pointed out, the two are essential to each other. Texts that tell us what to do must be supplemented by texts that tell us who we are and what we mean and what God is—more or less. But what has happened in Reform Judaism is that the aggadic texts have often been permitted to supersede the halachic texts, which is forbidden.

What Franz Rosenzweig called "aggadic doing" is forbidden—a refutation, I believe, of Reconstructionism, which reduces all laws to folkways. We cannot simply do more things in a random, self-searching, open-ended direction. That way, it seems to me, we miss the whole point of real doing, which should be pointed toward the service of God. Fundamental is *ma'aseh*, to do, not simply to talk (*midrash*) about doing. The Torah is mostly *nomos* (law), and where it is narrative, it is a narrative in which *nomos* is embedded. We Jews begin, according to Abraham Heschel, with a leap of action, not a leap of faith: First we *do*, then we believe. Reform Judaism must surrender once and for all any elements of a fatal Pauline anomism that denies value to obedience and it must accept Jewish authenticity. The test case for this will be gender issues, where we have not done well so far. Most of our thinking has been in the direction of recovery of tradition. With gender issues, for very good reasons, we have often felt offended by tradition, and so we have felt free simply to bypass the mitzvot as they have come to us. That, it seems to me, will not succeed. There may be a way, there must be a way, of making the Torah fully ethical because the rabbis said it has to be—*tov v'yashar*—but it cannot be simply by bracketing sacred texts in favor of some modernist gender presuppositions. Holiness is nonviolent self-transcendence, not secular political action. Our conscience must "relativize" modern ethical preferences—or make them holy.

It is fair to ask how, in this reading, we respond to the ultra-Orthodox who know exactly what God wants of us and have no hesitation in telling us that we are sinners for not doing what they do. Is it true to respond only that we are not yet able to do all of the commandments, but that in principle we would like to be what they are now? Of course, we cannot imagine that. We cannot wish that we were like Jewish "fundamentalists" who are invariably hard-line on Israel's keeping all the territories now occupied and glory in other self-serving, chauvinist deeds that they claim to be required by Torah. We do not want to be what they want us to be. We do not think God wants us to be like them.

Maybe God does not want them to be like them either. When we carefully and reverently study the Torah, we do not find in it exactly what they do. We find a dialectical, metaethical system of legislation that never permits us to do what is clearly wrong just because a biblical verse or a *halachah* seems to require it. We do not understand Torah literally or simplistically or narrowly. We nonetheless believe that we are reading it under God. We believe that the dangerously patriarchal in Torah is subserved under a more powerful command to love our neighbor as ourselves. Equality trumps male claims. We will not ever return to a system that advantages men or that disparages women, not because we are politically correct but because we are Jews. On the other hand, we are suspicious of permissive sexual leniencies (hetero- or homosexual) that make things all too easy for us. The Torah does not let us do whatever we feel like doing. We must wrestle with its stringencies as with its heroic humanness. What is modern is not always right, though we know we can never wholly escape our own time and place, nor are we required to do so.

We are obedient, but to the deepest and hardest sayings of the Law, not to its easiest or most apparently attractive ones. We must begin where we are—there is no other place to begin—without shame or inferiority. But, as we proceed in our knowledge of our faith, we must regularize our performance, leaving no possibility unexamined and no religious task untried. We shall never perform all of the mitzvot. No one does. But in our conscience we shall do the right as God gives us to see the right (as Lincoln said), without fear or favor, without stint or pride, without narrowness of vision nor an extravagant universalism under which nothing human would be real.

We are not trying to be Orthodox. We are trying to be Jewish. Terms such as *autonomy* or *freedom* no longer instruct our sensibilities. We are prepared to go back, far past where our Reform forebears ever went, neither idolizing nor disparaging what they have left us as a heritage.

A pious and modest hasidic rebbe died and was succeeded by his son, who built a mansion where he lived extravagantly. A disciple once asked him, "Why are you not more like your father?" "I am," the young rebbe responded. "He did not imitate and I do not imitate."

I conclude with the view of Emmanuel Levinas that engaged responsibility is prior to freedom. We come into the world already obligated by the mere gaze of the other, a gaze that demands from us a response. And, therefore, mitzvah, in a way—like all of ethics—is a kind of optics. It is a way of seeing the world. We must learn to see our world as Jews, responding to God. With all our heart and soul and might. Or—die trying.

A Summary: Ten Commandments

1. All of Judaism is mitzvah (Kushner: "response").
2. Reform Judaism has always affirmed mitzvot, in principle and practice.
3. We must ritualize the ethical and ethicize the ritual (e.g., Shabbat).
4. We cannot (re-)constitute the obligatory; we can only discover it.
5. We must recover all of tradition that we can.
6. We are guiltless about what we cannot (yet) retrieve.
7. Congregations and movements have as their chief purpose to assist in families' recovery of Torah.
8. Personal direction, not the number of mitzvot, is decisive.
9. We begin with "a leap of action" (Heschel), not "a leap of faith" (Kierkegaard).
10. "It is better to do because you are commanded than because you want to do it."

A Reform View of Mitzvot

ERIC H. YOFFIE

God, Torah, and Israel are the pillars upon which all of Judaism is built, the foundations of our past, the guarantors that our people will endure to the end of time. The great challenge of Jewish life at this moment is to reestablish a proper balance among these anchors of our tradition. For the modern movements of Judaism, crisis inevitably results when one dimension of Jewish life is emphasized at the expense of or to the exclusion of the others. For most of the post-Emancipation era, for example, modern Orthodoxy has focused almost exclusively on Torah, while paying only meager attention to God and Israel. And the result, in many instances, has been disaster: a religious behaviorism devoid of the leavening influences of compassion, spirituality, and Jewish peoplehood.

Reform Judaism, on the other hand, began as a God-intoxicated movement, or so I conclude from my reading of early Reform literature. But Torah and Israel were less in evidence. More recently, we have turned to Torah, but in an exceedingly selective way. Too often *tefillah* (prayer) and the rituals of home observance have been ignored, while our commitment to *tikkun olam* (mending the world) has been separated from the texts and values of our tradition and from the commanding voice of God.

But how are we to attain the balance that we seek? We will do so by the wholehearted embrace of mitzvah as the organizing principle of Reform Judaism. It is the mitzvah-intoxicated Reform Jew who will be the agent of a serious religious revival in our movement. What is a mitzvah-intoxicated Reform Jew? It is a Reform Jew who observes precepts of Torah because they are commanded by God, and who, in al-most every instance, seeks a supportive community of liberal Jews to stand by him in his observance.

If we have Jews who are immersed in mitzvah—who speak its lan-guage, understand its nuances, and struggle with its meaning—then we will have Jews who understand the interplay among God, Torah, and Israel, and who appreciate what difference it makes for us to con-tinue as a distinctive group. Mitzvah is the key. We all know that the tenuous bonds of anti-anti-Semitism, a sense of shared history, a feel-ing for ethnicity, and a concern for the welfare of Israel and the safety of Jews elsewhere are each insufficient to insure the continuity of the Jewish people. We cannot survive on so slender a base.

What is required for a revival of mitzvah in our midst? First, a clear understanding of what mitzvah is:

- A mitzvah is a religious act, drawn from Torah, that is carried out by Jews who believe that these acts have been transmitted to us by a commanding God and that they are indicative of the Comman-der's power to command.

- Mitzvah is a reflection of Judaism's insistence on concretizing ethics and theology into daily practice.

- Mitzvah is the natural, logical, and necessary extension of Jewish faith, which becomes meaningful only when we ask: "What does my belief demand of me?" For the Jew, this is always the critical question.

- Mitzvah is the instrument by which we infuse life with the holy. For centuries we have been secularizing the world, clearing it of God the way that forested land is stripped for paving. It is mitzvah that enables us to sacralize the God-forsaken places in the lives of Jews.

- Mitzvah is our connection with Sinai. God revealed the Torah to the Jewish people at Sinai, and however we may understand that event, I know that somehow, in some way, I was there. Somehow, in some way, my DNA was present in the crowd. Performing a mitzvah takes us back to the sacred mountain.

- Mitzvah connects us to God. A hasidic commentary associates the word mitzvah with the Aramaic word *tsavta*, meaning "togetherness." A mitzvah is the act that joins together the Jew and God.

- Mitzvah is the heart of Torah because without commandments, there is no Torah.

Second, a revival of mitzvah requires a clear understanding of what mitzvah is not:

Mitzvot are not identical with rituals, sancta, or minhagim (customs). All these things may have value and a place in our Jewish lives. But a custom, even a time-honored and history-sanctioned custom, is not a mitzvah. This is a matter of some importance because we live in an era of reritualization. At this moment, many North Americans, Jews and non-Jews, share a deep craving for meaningful ritual that connects them with one another, that marks the passages of their lives, and that evokes a sense of wonder about human existence. Many of our congregants are prepared to celebrate ritual because it affirms common patterns, values, and the shared joys, risks, and sorrows of life. This search is positive and welcome in every way; surely we as rabbis have something to offer here. If Jews are seeking out some form of transcendence and believe that ritual channels are the best means of making this connection, then we are obligated to draw from our tradition to assist them in their search. But my word of warning is this: Customs, ancient or modern, that are put forward to meet immediate needs and that are regularly discarded if the response is not satisfactory, must not be confused with mitzvot, which by their very nature are lasting and divinely mandated.

The confusions of definition and the importance of clarification emerge clearly from the discussion in the CCAR's *Gates of Mitzvah*, published in 1979. This volume contains four essays on the meaning of mitzvah, contributed by Roland Gittelsohn, David Polish, and Arthur Lelyveld, *zichronam livracha*, and Herman Schaalman, *yibadel l'chayim*. Rabbis Gittelsohn, Polish, and Lelyveld were all great leaders of our movement, and Roland Gittelsohn in particular was a friend, teacher, and mentor to me. Yet what was fascinating about their essays was their affirmation of the existence of a *metzaveh* (divine commander) and then their willingness to define away the term into meaninglessness. If the authority behind a mitzvah lies primarily in history and not in God, is it a mitzvah? If the authority lies primarily in the people and not in God, is it a mitzvah? A mitzvah is a Jewish affirmation in which there is a human element, to be sure—and I will have more to say about this presently—but its uniqueness flows from the fact that in carrying out the action we feel the touch of *Shechinah* (Divine Presence), and it thus evokes in us religious wonder.

My point is that mitzvah cannot become an all-purpose term for any Jewish action that we choose to do, for virtually any reason. We need to beware of taking religious categories that are absolutely unique and reducing them to other categories that have no application. In this regard, Mordecai Kaplan should be our teacher: Kaplan called upon us to do Jewish acts for historical, ethnic, and naturalist reasons, but he realized that acts so understood are not mitzvot and should not be so called.

The essay in the group with which I most identified was the one by Herman Schaalman, who articulated the *sui generis* nature of mitzvah and insisted that it not be explained in terms of other factors or considerations. Rabbi Schaalman made the point plain: An embrace of mitzvah means that I accept God as my commander, that I am prepared to live my life in response to God and as God's covenant partner. Rabbi Schaalman is correct: If a discussion of mitzvot is to be meaningful, this needs to be our starting point.

Third, a revival of mitzvah requires that we deal honestly with the issue of individual conscience and personal autonomy. Our movement has elevated the individual to a position of supreme importance, and we have enshrined the individual conscience as our final authority. If mitzvah becomes the central religious category of Reform Jewish life, does that mean that we do away with individual autonomy?

Of course not. It has been true and will remain true that every Jew can pick and choose which mitzvot to observe and which not to observe. That is simply a self-evident fact of modern Jewish life. Nonetheless, I do believe that we need a crucial shift in emphasis.

Our message should be this: Reform Judaism is a religion of personal commitment and personal responsibility, a religion that requires immersion in Torah, a religion that connects the Jew to God through mitzvot that reflect God's commanding voice. Reform Jews aspire to be commanded; failing to be commanded, they cannot be religiously fulfilled or religiously complete. Do we make our own choices? Of course.

But let us be clear: Reform Judaism is a religious discipline that requires a great deal of us and in return promises to transform our lives. But the starting point needs to be a focus on mitzvah and on our obligation to be observant Jews. And leadership—in particular rabbinic leadership—has a special responsibility to bring about this change of direction.

Fourth, a revival of mitzvah requires that we be honest about the difficulty of introducing mitzvot into our lives. It is difficult to embrace mitzvot because this requires that we recognize God. But if, in Heschel's words, God is a mass of vagueness behind a veil of enigmas, and if God's voice has become alien to our minds, hearts, and souls, and if we have learned to listen to every "I" except the "I" of God, then there can be no mitzvah. Mitzvah requires God. And from this it follows that if mitzvot are done for the sake of God, we must be prepared, at least some of the time, to please God before we please ourselves. But this is not simple in a culture where self-gratification and "feel-good" religion are guiding principles.

Even for those in our midst who are able to connect with God and to feel commanded, they will not feel commanded every moment. Inspirations are brief, sporadic, and rare. There will therefore be a temptation—a strong temptation—to observe mitzvot sporadically, episodically, only at those moments when the soul enters into accord with the spirit. The answer to this, of course, is religious routine, religious habit. Since we can feel commanded only some of the time, and since inspiration is not something that we can acquire once and for all, we are challenged to enter into a routine that holds us in readiness for God's commanding voice. We are challenged, on the basis of occasional inspiration, to feel the urgency of answering God's command even when we hear the commanding voice as weak and faint. But, alas, our people are impatient, easily distracted, and unaccustomed to the discipline that routine requires. "Mitzvot will make you holy," we can tell them. But they will not be easily convinced.

Some Reform Jews might respond to my remarks with alarm, as a rejection of Reform principles, as warmed-over Orthodoxy, as the sort of *neo-frumkeit* that seems to be so fashionable nowadays in some circles. Some of them might, but they would be wrong. What I have said is quintessentially Reform because to be a Reform Jew means that you do not take every word of the Torah as the literal expression of God's will, and you do not support an unreflective adherence to tradition.

I believe that there are general principles to which serious Jews of all types would subscribe: revelation, a chosen people, a code of conduct that embodies Jewish singularity, and the desire not to be like everyone else. We would all agree that it is Torah that binds us to a shared life, a shared history, and a shared destiny and that Judaism cannot survive the dissolution of that essence. But on the operative level, the differences between Reform Jews and Orthodox Jews remain fairly clear. For Orthodox Jews, the starting point is *halachah*—commitment to a system of law and a body of mitzvot that takes precedence over analysis or discussion of any particular mitzvah. For Reform Jews, such an approach is impossible. We can be halachic only in the general sense that we should feel a need to adopt an all-embracing approach to religious life. But let us be clear. *Halachah*, as a normative term, refers to acceptance of a legal system comprised of a body of law, every element of which binds and obligates the Jewish people. So understood, the notion of a Reform *halachah* is contrary, I believe, to Reform principles. Reform Jews too are obligated by the law, but for us, the operative category is mitzvah. We can be, and should be, mitzvah-directed Jews and mitzvah-inspired Jews, but what this means is that we make our decisions one mitzvah at a time.

And how do we do that? Let me answer that question. A mitzvah, as I have said, is not a divine fiat. It is an encounter between God and Jew, originating—metaphorically, at least—at Mount Sinai and involving two players: on the one hand, a divine commander—a *metzaveh*, and on the other hand, Moses, who was the *metzuveh*—who experienced himself as being commanded, summoned, and directed. For a mitzvah to exist, there must always be both sides of the equation—the one who commands and the one who is commanded. And since both are involved, that is why our Torah is known both as *Torat Adonai* and *Torat Moshe*. In referring to Moses, of course, I am referring both to Moses and to all his spiritual descendants—the prophets, the rabbis, and the teachers who saw themselves to be divinely commanded or divinely inspired, who fashioned our tradition, and who passed it on to subsequent generations. Our Torah is a record of conversations between God and Moses and God and the people Israel; it is a record of God talking to Israel and Israel talking to God. Both the Written and the Oral Torah reverberate with the divine-human encounter. And out of this conversation, recorded in our sacred texts, we extract the mitzvot, which give direction to our lives.

The key to understanding mitzvah is understanding the relationship between commander and commanded: Why did Moses respond as he did to the divine command? Why did he hear what he heard at Sinai, when someone else might have heard the message differently, or perhaps might have heard nothing at all? We cannot answer these questions with certainty, since revelation is fundamentally a mystery. Still, we assume that three factors influenced the response of Moses to God: first, the personal spiritual makeup of Moses; second, the historical conditions of the period in which he lived; and third, the nature of the Jewish people in his time. After all, the Jew responds to God not only as an individual but as a member of a religious community.

Having said this, we realize that different Jews at different times will necessarily respond in different ways to the *metzaveh*, the divine commander. You and I will respond differently than Moses responded. We are different people, with different experiences, backgrounds, and spiritual qualities.

The historical conditions of Moses' time gave rise to a certain type of response. But now that those conditions have radically changed, we will find that the response of Moses may no longer be comprehensible to us; it may have lost its binding force. Furthermore, because we are a product of the community in which we live, the dynamics of Jewish life today will greatly influence our reaction to the divine command.

What is extraordinary, of course, is how frequently the divine command, as recorded in Torah and the sacred literature of Judaism, evokes from us precisely the same response that it evoked from Moses and the Jewish people in the biblical, rabbinical, and medieval periods. Many of the mitzvot in the biblical books, for example, are as powerful and inspiring for us when we read them today as they were for the people of Israel in an earlier era. Yet as Reform Jews we also recognize that often we do not respond as Moses did, and we cannot be *metzuvim*—we cannot be commanded as he was commanded. In those cases we must say plainly: What was a mitzvah for Moses cannot be a mitzvah for us.

And who is the ultimate authority? Who ultimately determines whether a precept recorded in Torah is mitzvah and is binding on the Reform Jew? This question I have already answered: The individual decides. We rely here on the words of Martin Buber: "I must distinguish," he wrote, "in my innermost being, between what is commanded me and what is not commanded me." This is both a central precept of Reform Judaism and also an objective description of reality in modern Jewish life. There is much that we can do to encourage observance, but in the final analysis, it is the individual who decides. There is no coercive power in Reform Jewish life that can decide for us.

But the danger of course does not come from the remote possibility that our rabbinate will rise up and attempt to impose a Reform *halachah* on an unwilling and rebellious membership. The danger comes from the opposite direction: from an absurd reductionism that suggests that having jettisoned so many mitzvot we can jettison them all and replace them with less demanding categories of religious practice; that sees in Torah an absolute maximum of interpretation and an absolute minimum of revelation; that celebrates a religious revival that is more style than substance, turning away from those elements of mitzvah and *kedushah* (holiness) that have so long and so universally exercised their hold on the Jewish soul.

How can we bring a commitment to mitzvah to our synagogues? How do we infuse Reform Jewish life with mitzvah-consciousness? We know that this cannot be done by decree because we know the realities of North American Jewish life. What has dominated North American Judaism for the last century is human needs, not divine commands—American integration, not Jewish chosenness. In the eyes of too many of our congregants, Jews do not exist to serve Judaism; Judaism exists to serve the needs of Jews. Of course, there is no reason why we should not expect our human and personal needs to be met in a synagogue setting. But my point is that our culture is not necessarily conducive to a revival of mitzvah. When the synagogue has become an institution of ethnicity rather than religious expression, and theology has become the handmaid of sociology, then the integrity of mitzvah is necessarily in doubt. Nonetheless, I see enough that is encouraging in our midst to make me optimistic. While this is necessarily a broader topic, it seems to me that there are several paths that might ultimately lead us in the right direction.

As an undergraduate at Brandeis University, an agnostic and a committed ethnic Jew, I began studying Hebrew and immersed myself in serious text study for the first time. I was then totally indifferent to Shabbat, at best a very occasional *daven*er. But the mysteries of Hebrew and the excitement of the Genesis stories, read for the first time in the original, led me to a discovery: Torah study was not just a practical tool. It was an inspiration, a great adventure, a source of joy. It was, in fact, another means of gazing at eternity—an act of communion with the sacred. When I came to the legal sections of Torah, they possessed a coherence and a compelling power that I had not experienced previously. Reading the Hebrew words, I felt a humility in the face of mystery—a stirring, a response, and even a sense of obedience in the presence of the divine word. For the first time in my life, I felt commanded.

Others, just perhaps, may find their way to mitzvah through Hebrew language and study of text. And I believe too that even if the modern Jew seeks community and not command, very often community will lead to command. We know that Sinai was an experience of the entire people—a communal transformation, rather than that of an individual. Our religion is that of a people. As Arthur Green has reminded us, there is no reclaiming the silent sounds or the holy moments of Sinai without also reclaiming as our own the people of Sinai, as distanced as they may be from the foot of that sacred mountain. And it works the other way as well. When we love and embrace the entire Jewish people, when we seek and build community, we are often drawn to the sacred energy of Sinai and to the commandments given on top of the mountain. And most important of all is rabbinic leadership.

I am reminded of the story of the golden calf. The Children of Israel had just been liberated from Egypt. As they wandered through the desert, Moses had been their leader, guide, arbiter, and judge. But then Moses ascended Mount Sinai to meet with God and to receive the Law. With Moses gone, the Israelites found themselves suddenly conflicted. They were exhilarated by their newfound freedom; but at the same time, their unexpected independence imposed upon them an extreme and debilitating anxiety. At that point, according to the Talmud, Satan tricked them into thinking that Moses was dead. With their leader gone, the Israelites very quickly became panic-stricken and out of control, and the golden calf was created as an attempt to replace him. We face, in a sense, a similar challenge. For most of our people, the *halachah* has collapsed, traditional sources of authority have been undermined, and community discipline has been weakened. We are free, but we are also worried because we have no Moses to guide us. What is essential now, I would suggest, is a Reform rabbinate that does not take refuge in religious language that is deliberately vague and ambiguous; what is essential is a Reform rabbinate that speaks and feels a language of covenant and commandment, a Reform rabbinate that is committed to Sinai and that can still feel the glow of those moments when we glimpsed the warmth of God's light.

Do not misunderstand me: We are modern Jews, creative in our approach to the society and culture in which we live, willing to experiment with various forms of Jewish renewal, open to critical scholarship and all else that we might profitably exploit to enhance our understanding of Jewish tradition. We know that the word of God is multivalent and multivocal. But this too we know: It is still the word of God; It is still God's commanding voice; and mitzvah is God's instrument that transforms what happened at Sinai into a way of life and a religious destiny.

Recovering the Hidden Torah:
A Mystical Paradigm for Mitzvah

LAWRENCE A. ENGLANDER

Imagine that you are visited by a friend who has never heard of the game of baseball. You take this friend to a game, hoping she will enjoy it, but all you receive for your efforts is a look of consternation. "Why is everyone wearing pajamas?" she asks. "Why does the man in the mask keep sending people away? Why do they keep running around in counterclockwise circles?" Patiently, you try to explain: "You will understand once you know the rules of the game. Then it will all make sense."

Just as this statement is true for baseball, it also applies to traditional Jewish practice. To many of us, the behavior of halachically observant Jews evokes similar consternation. "Why can't you carry your house key in your pocket on Shabbat? Why do you need ten adult Jews in order to say certain prayers? Why can't you eat chicken with milk?" A halachically observant Jew could give the same reply we gave to our friend: "You will understand once you know the rules of the game. Then it will all make sense." But that is only part of the answer. In traditional Judaism, the rules of the game are the mitzvot, the divine commandments recorded in the Torah and rabbinic texts. Behind the mitzvot is a rationale as to why all the rules are invested with divine authority. If we accept that rationale, then all the rules fit together into the intricately organized system of *halachah.*

The problem for many of us is that the traditional rationale behind the mitzvot no longer makes sense to us. But neither have we been able to develop a new one upon which everyone will agree. As Reform Jews, we sometimes perceive ourselves standing in a baseball diamond where all the bases are still in position[1] but some of the equipment is redesigned, some players wander randomly over the field, and sometimes the umpire's calls are ignored. If the essence of the game itself keeps changing, how can we know which rules to follow? How can we play the game at all?

Our task, then, is to discover a new rationale that will make sense for liberal Jews. In essence, what we seek is a *paradigm* for mitzvah. To begin this search, it will help us to understand why the traditional one no longer works for many of us. Then we shall examine one attempt in Reform Jewish history to revise the rationale and discover why it, too, has failed. Finally, we shall try to develop a framework within which a new set of rules may evolve.

The Rabbinic Paradigm

First, we turn to the traditional paradigm, developed by the rabbis over two thousand years ago. The "rabbinic paradigm" can be broken down into the following components:

God gave the Written Torah[2] to Moses on Mount Sinai. It has been transmitted to us through an unbroken chain of tradition from Moses to the present.

God has already revealed, in the Written Torah, everything we need to know for all time. The prophetic revelation is now complete, so that even rules regarding space travel and organ transplants are already embedded in Scripture.

God has also given us the Oral Torah, a set of reasoning tools by which we can extract what we need to know from the Written Torah. When we want to know what God wants us to do (i.e., how we are to observe mitzvot) in our own time, we apply these

---

1: As a playful suggestion, the three bases are the three pillars upon which the world stands *(Mishnah Avot 1:2)*: Torah (study), *avodah* (prayer), and *gemilut chasadim* (good deeds). Home plate is our messianic striving toward *tikkun olam* (the mending of the world).

2: By this term the rabbis mean the Five Books of Moses. By extension, the entire *Tanakh* (Hebrew Bible) is considered to be God's word.

tools to the text of the Written Torah and derive our response. Many such inquiries are already recorded in rabbinic texts such as the Talmud and *midrashim*, but we must keep in mind that the process has no end. Every time we engage in dialogue with a sacred text, we add to Oral Torah.

The rabbinic paradigm is a finely balanced system of insights, teachings, and laws that inspires our admiration the more we study it. Yet it is based upon certain assumptions that many liberal Jews find difficult, if not impossible, to accept. First of all, it assumes that God is the author of the entire Written Torah. Biblical scholarship, however, has cast serious doubt upon this postulate.[3] Second, history plays no significant role in the rabbinic paradigm; what was considered to be ideal human behavior for Abraham and Sarah remains the same for us today.[4] In contrast, Reform Judaism has generally considered divine revelation to be progressive—that is, as humanity grows and times change, our relationship with God will change, and therefore so will the mitzvot. If we can no longer accept the premises of the rabbinic paradigm, two alternatives remain. We can either behave as if the rules are still intact, or we can reexamine the assumptions of the rulebook itself.

The Progress Paradigm

The second alternative was taken by Rabbi Abraham Geiger, one of the most influential ideologues of Reform Judaism in nineteenth-century Europe. For the sake of our discussion, Geiger's model will be referred to as the "progress paradigm." [5] Geiger began with the assumption that the Torah was inspired by God but that the words themselves are of human authorship. The written record left by our biblical ancestors

3: See, for example, the summary by W. Gunther Plaut, "General Introduction to the Torah," in *The Torah: A Modern Commentary* (New York: Union of American Hebrew Congregations, 1981), xviii–xxv.

4: The rabbinic paradigm does allow for certain changes in circumstances. For example, since the Temple is destroyed we cannot offer sacrifices, even though it is a mitzvah in the Written Torah to do so. By the same token, sacrifice has not been revoked as a mitzvah but remains "on the books" until the Temple is rebuilt in the time of the Messiah.

5: For a more recent formulation of this paradigm, see Arthur J. Lelyveld, "Mitzvah: The Larger Context," in Simeon Maslin, ed., *Gates of Mitzvah* (New York: Central Conference of American Rabbis, 1979), 111–15.

certainly reflects eternal divine truths, but these truths are filtered through the perceptions of the authors' time and place in history. For example, the dietary laws, according to Geiger, were a means of keeping the people of Israel separate from the idolatrous Canaanites so that the Israelites' mission would not be compromised. The talmudic rabbis later extended these laws into a system for observing *kashrut*. But, for Geiger, the dietary laws are a "husk" designed to protect the "kernel" of monotheism until it was ready to grow of its own accord. He writes:

> The core is the pure faith in God. At a time when unbelief and superstition, idolatry, and nature worship were rampant everywhere, this core had to be enveloped in a mass of ceremonies, so that the pure spiritual treasure would not be crushed. But now spring has long since come into the life of mankind. All the civilized world has discarded primitive idol worship and the concepts of God and His worship have been refined. Hence, the spirit of Judaism now no longer needs this rough mantle; on the contrary . . . it must shed it in order to sow the seeds of its ideals that they may bear fruit in the total development of mankind.[6]

For Geiger, the tradition was no longer the sole arbiter of Jewish behavior. Two external criteria— reason and history—now enabled him and his followers to choose the mitzvot that had lasting value for them. By applying these two criteria, we progress closer and closer, in each generation, toward the true will of God.

This paradigm, too, is based upon assumptions. In the main, it presupposes that we can clearly distinguish between God's will and human interpretation in Scripture. For Geiger, the divine component lies in the moral principles of justice, goodness, and peace. He regards the ritual observances as means to an end, ceremonial practices that may inspire us toward ethical conduct. In cases where a ritual law runs the risk of becoming an end in itself, it is better, claims Geiger, to dispense with the husk than to let it choke the kernel. Geiger often quoted the biblical prophets Amos and Isaiah, who admonished the people that God cares much less for ritual sacrifice than for moral acts of righteousness toward our fellow human beings.

6: Abraham Geiger, "On Renouncing Judaism," in Max Weiner, *Abraham Geiger and Liberal Judaism* (Philadelphia: Jewish Publication Society of America, 1962), 286.

Whether they know it or not, many Jews invoke the progress paradigm when they say, "What Judaism really teaches us is how to be good human beings. The ritual acts are a matter of personal choice." If we take this paradigm to its logical conclusion, we face an intriguing dilemma. If God just wants us to be good, then why bother to remain Jewish? Since the moral principles of the Torah are now acknowledged by most of Western civilization—in fact, by most of the peoples of the world—would it not be easier for us to blend into the majority culture and shed the "husk" of Jewish tradition? Whereas the rabbinic paradigm may assume too much in its understanding of Written Torah, the progress paradigm assumes too little. Can we find a paradigm that affirms the unique nature of the Jewish people and also incorporates our sensitivity to reason and history?

The Paradigm of the Hidden Tablets

In an attempt to develop such a paradigm, we shall concentrate upon one story in the Written Torah and the interpretations that emanate from it. Exodus 32 records that Moses came down from Mount Sinai carrying the two tablets of the Ten Commandments "inscribed on both their surfaces, inscribed on one side and on the other" (Exod. 32:15). When he saw the people dancing round the golden calf, "he became enraged; he hurled the tablets from his hands and shattered them at the foot of the mountain" (32:19). Thus the tablets were destroyed, and later Moses was summoned by God to make a second set (Exod. 34:1).

In the literature of *midrash,* the rabbis elaborate upon this story.[7] When the holy letters of the two tablets came into contact with the sin of the calf, they flew back to heaven to maintain their purity. What had previously been the work of God weightlessly accompanying Moses down the mountain now became two heavy stones in his hands, which he subsequently dropped.

The rabbis then address the question, What was the difference between the first set of tablets and the second? One *midrash* proposes the following answer:

7: See B. T., *Pesachim* 87b.

Moses was upset about the shattering of the tablets until the Holy Blessed One said to him, "Do not be upset about the first set of tablets, which contained only the Ten Commandments. On the second set of tablets I shall also give you laws, interpretations, and legends."

(*Exodus Rabbah* 46:1)

According to this *midrash*, the second set of tablets contained not only the Written Torah but the Oral Torah as well.[8] In order to guide us through an imperfect world, God gave us a tool to understand and apply the Written Torah.

This theme is further embellished in a passage from the Zohar, the compendium of Jewish mystical teachings written in thirteenth-century Spain.[9] This passage poses an interesting question: When the second set of tablets was given to Moses after the golden calf incident, were they an exact replica of the first set or was something missing from them? The Zohar addresses this question:

At the time when the Holy Blessed One wished to give the Torah to Israel, the tablets were inscribed frontwards and backwards. As Scripture states, "inscribed on one side and on the other (Exod. 32:15). . . . This is because before Israel made the calf, God wished to give two Torahs—that is, Written and Oral—through Moses to Israel. . . . But when they made the calf, the letters flew away from two sides. . . .Thereupon "he [Moses] shattered them [the tablets] at the foot of the mountain" (Exod. 32:19). The Torah flew away from there and said, "I went away full, and now the Eternal has brought me back empty" (Ruth 1:21).

(*Midrash HaNe elam* to the Book of Ruth,
in *Zohar Chadash* 83b–d)

8: It is possible to interpret this *midrash* as a polemic against the Christian teaching that the Written Torah is now abrogated so that only the Ten Commandments need be followed. The *midrash* explains that the Oral Torah, too, is sent by God and is therefore binding.

9: For more information on the Zohar and its authorship, see Daniel C. Matt, *Zohar: The Book of Enlightenment* (New York, Ramsey, Toronto: Paulist Press, 1982), especially the introduction.

Because the people were not ready for the "full" Torah in the first set of tablets, God withdraws part of it and leaves our ancestors with a fragmented, incomplete Torah. The Zohar comes to the opposite conclusion of the above *midrash* in *Exodus Rabbah*: It was the first set of tablets that contained both Written and Oral Torah.[10] The second set— the one we have now—has only the Oral Torah. Therefore, there is no Written Torah in our world! Even the Five Books of Moses fall into the category of Oral Torah.[11]

As this Zohar passage continues to unfold,[12] it develops this theme into some fascinating variations by comparing the literary images in Exodus 32 to the tragic story of Naomi in the Book of Ruth. Both stories share the following motifs:

Sets of pairings. Just as Naomi was blessed with a loving husband, Elimelech, so were the Written and Oral Torahs coupled together in the *first set* of tablets. Elimelech and Naomi lived in Bethlehem (the Hebrew *bet lechem* means "house of bread"); for the people of Israel, Mount Sinai was their house of "bread" or sustenance, since that is where they received Torah.

A tragic loss. Just as Naomi becomes widowed and also loses her two sons while living in Moab, a land of idolatry, so does Israel lose the first set of tablets by making the golden calf, an idol.

A sense of incompleteness but with hope of reintegration. When Naomi returns with her daughter-in-law Ruth to Bethlehem, she feels empty since she is bereft of husband, home, and sustenance; it is through the later marriage of Ruth to Boaz, Naomi's kinsman, that the family is reconstituted and Naomi regains her status within her people. Similarly, when the Ten Commandments return to Mount Sinai in the form of the second set of tablets, they,

---

10: For the Zohar, the two Torahs reflect two aspects of God. For the reader who is familiar with the system of *sefirot*, the Written Torah is the *sefirah Tiferet* and the Oral Torah is *Malchut/Shechinah*. As a result of the shattered tablets, we are not only bereft of a complete Torah, but we also suffer a diminished revelation of God.

11: For a discussion of this notion, see Gershom Scholem, *On the Kabbalah and Its Symbolism* (New York: Schocken Books, 1969), 47–50.

12: For a more complete discussion of this passage, see Lawrence A. Englander, *The Mystical Study of Ruth* (Atlanta: Scholars Press, 1993), especially the translation and commentary to section 12, "The Two Torahs."

too, are incomplete. Recalling that Boaz redeemed Ruth, that this couple were the ancestors of King David, who in turn is to be the progenitor of the Messiah, the mystics of the Zohar engaged upon a parallel quest to redeem the Written Torah and bring it back into the world to reunite it with the Oral Torah.

Consequences of the Paradigm of the Hidden Tablets

If we take this model as our rationale for observing mitzvot, we find some significant implications. First of all, the paradigm of the hidden tablets teaches that the Torah in our possession does not contain the complete expression of God's will. Since we lack the corrective of the first set of tablets, some of the mitzvot in our present Torah may strike us as tentative, contradictory, or even incomprehensible. There may also be other mitzvot that are not yet recorded, because it is up to us to discover them. This approach to Torah lacks the confident certainty of the other two paradigms; since the Torah is incomplete—and so we are, too—different interpretations of Scripture are possible and hence different personal patterns of mitzvot. This makes it difficult for us as liberal Jews to develop universally accepted "rules of the game." But this paradigm also offers an advantage. Through the metaphor of the tablets, it teaches that the apprehension of God's will is more complex than simply reading a written record, however sacred. The infusion of Divine Presence into our world depends not only upon our reception of it but also upon our active participation in interpreting it. Thus our paradigm allows for historical development and change, something we consider important in our observance of mitzvot.

A second consequence of our condition is that we are also cautioned to exercise humility. Although we have only the Oral Torah, the second set of tablets, in our possession, it is Torah nonetheless. However fragmented it may be, it is our only access to the Written Torah, which is still hidden. We must preserve as much of this fragmented Torah as we can so that we may ultimately complete it. At times, the exercise of reason may assist us in deciphering a perplexing biblical passage or rabbinic law. But at other times, we are summoned to venture humbly into unknown territory, with the faith that our tentative steps will lead us to firm ground. In his discussion on Jewish observance, Rabbi Abraham Joshua Heschel wrote about a "leap of action" that can propel us into faith:

> A Jew is asked to take a leap of action rather than a leap of thought. He is asked to surpass his needs, to do more than he understands in order to understand more than he does. In carrying out the word of the Torah he is ushered into the presence of spiritual meaning. Through the ecstasy of deeds he learns to be certain of the hereness of God. Right living is a way to right thinking.[13]

The paradigm of the hidden tablets stands in marked contrast to Geiger's image of "kernel and husk." For Geiger, we must discard the husk and preserve the kernel. For the hidden tablets paradigm, the kernel is at present beyond our apprehension; since the husk leads us to the kernel, its instructions must be preserved, even when they cannot be fully rationalized. Rather than bend the Torah to our needs and circumstances, we must strive to stretch ourselves toward the hidden Torah. Therefore, this paradigm has a conserving element to it. The onus is not upon the Torah to convince us to follow its teachings; rather, it is incumbent upon us to justify any diversion from the specifications of Jewish tradition. Before we abandon any practice, we must first be prepared to ask, "Is there any good reason why I should *not* observe this?"

There are several instances where we do possess good reasons for departing from Scripture. One main principle, which evolved in later periods of Jewish history, is that of egalitarianism. Since we consider other nations and religions to be equal to ourselves in God's eyes, we do not condone the genocide of any people, despite the reference to the Canaanites in Deuteronomy 20:10–18.[14] Since we regard all Jews as equal under the law, most liberal Jews no longer accord special ritual privileges to the descendants of the tribe of Levi. And because sex-

---

13: Abraham Joshua Heschel, *God in Search of Man* (New York: Harper and Row, 1955), 283.

14: Reading this passage with an understanding of its history, we may view it as a "retrospective command." (See the commentary of W.G. Plaut to Deut. 20:16 in *The Torah: A Modern Commentary*.) Since the Canaanite nations were vexing the kingdom of Israel, the authors of Deuteronomy may have engaged in some wishful thinking: "Had the generation of Joshua slaughtered the Canaanites, we would not have to worry about them now!" This approach allows us to understand statements in the Torah without necessarily justifying them.

ual equality is now a fundamental principle of Reform Judaism, men and women in our movement share identical religious obligations. Other applications of this principle, however, are less clear cut. For example, proponents of the progress paradigm often argue that Jewish garments of prayer place an artificial barrier between Jews and Gentiles; for the sake of equality, then, they should be discarded. But one can also view *kipa, tallit,* and *tefillin* as uniquely Jewish modes of prayer without necessarily claiming any superiority for the wearers. The Torah in our possession, since it is entirely Oral Law in this paradigm, remains open to discussion.

Along with the conserving element, a third consequence of this paradigm shows its dynamic character as well. If the ultimate Torah is still hidden, our quest for it will involve not only a regaining of lost wisdom but also the discovery of new insights. The Judaism that evolves from this paradigm, while recapturing many neglected traditions, will essentially be something innovative and different from anything we have seen before. For example, a careful rereading of rabbinic texts regarding God's role in the healing process along with mystical meditation techniques and contemporary insights in medicine and psychology have combined in the development of healing services that depart from the traditional liturgy and offer yet another approach to prayer.

The quest for the hidden Torah is not a solitary endeavor; it is a collective effort. Therefore, a fourth consequence of this paradigm is that we shall have to reevaluate the "rugged individualism" that Reform Jews often bring to Judaism. There are times when I must be willing to place the needs and wishes of my community over my personal autonomy, my right to choose for myself. This does not mean to say that the community should have the power to *compel* me to abide by a particular observance; rather, I freely consent to sacrifice some autonomy for the sake of a communal principle. Immanuel Kant, a philosopher often quoted by Geiger and proponents of the progress paradigm, never considered autonomy to mean "I can do whatever I want." Autonomy, for him, was "the capacity of the will . . . to act in accordance with universal law."[15] In other words, we acknowledge that sometimes our obligations to the community actually define our individual preferences. One

---

15: Theodore M. Greene, "The Historical Context and Religious Significance of Kant's *Religion,*" introduction to Immanuel Kant, *Religion within the Limits of Reason Alone* (New York: Harper Torchbooks, 1960), lxxxiii. I am indebted to Professor Kenneth Seeskin for this insight.

example may illustrate this notion. When people become Jews by choice, we welcome them not only into our Reform community but into the entire people of Israel. To demonstrate our belonging to *klal Yisrael*, should our converts not be required to observe the traditional rites of *milah* and *mikveh*?[16]

Before we proceed further, this paradigm may be sounding a warning bell for some students of Jewish history. In the seventeenth century, a self-proclaimed messiah named Shabbetai Tzvi propounded a similar notion of two Torahs. The Torah in our possession, he claimed, comes from the Tree of Knowledge in the Garden of Eden and is riddled with dichotomies: distinguishing between good and evil, permissible and forbidden, true and false. But with the coming of the Messiah (who, of course, was Shabbetai himself), a new Torah would be revealed to the Jewish people, a Torah that emanated from the elusive Tree of Life. This new Torah would seem to contradict the older Torah, but the "enlightened" would understand that Shabbetai's Torah was meant for a new age of spiritually elevated people. Critics of Shabbetai Tzvi pointed out that this new, progressive Torah of Life encouraged people to commit adultery, break the Sabbath, and utter blasphemies against God. Once we abandon the mitzvot, the critics claimed, we become open targets for such licentiousness and anarchy. Could the paradigm of the hidden tablets lead us down the same crooked path as the Sabbateans?

I believe there are significant differences between the paradigm of the hidden tablets and the teachings of Shabbetai Tzvi. The Sabbatean doctrine sought to nullify the present Torah and replace it with another, one of Shabbetai's own devising. In our model, we seek not a replacement but a reintegration. By claiming that our Torah is not yet complete, we acknowledge that its teachings are still evolving; this is a far cry from Sabbatean antinomianism. Furthermore, Sabbateanism was a totalitarian movement demanding unswerving obedience to its leader. In our paradigm, every Jew is an essential part of the quest, and therefore communal dialogue and consensus are essential components of the process.

16: See Jakob Petuchowski, "Plural Models within the Halakhah," in *Judaism*, Winter 1970, 77–89. Petuchowski argues that the decision whether to observe a particular *halachah* should depend on who is affected by it. He outlines three distinct spheres of individual, community and Jewish people; see especially pp. 83f.

Practical Applications

It is not sufficient to discuss mitzvah in theory. We must also determine how any theoretical model will spell itself out in our daily lives as Jews. How, then, will our quest for the hidden tablets affect our Jewish behavior? The three examples below have been chosen because they illustrate the dynamic character of this paradigm. While each of these mitzvot has its roots in Jewish tradition, our generation is exploring new modes of observing them.

Daily Prayer. Three times every day—*Shacharit, Mincha,* and *Ma'ariv*—it is a mitzvah to pray from the Siddur either with a congregation or by oneself. In addition, there are blessings to be said before and after meals, as well as a list of *birchot nehenin*[17] to acknowledge various events. It is fair to say that this regimen of daily prayer is not a regular part of most of our lives. I, for one, can find many reasons why I am unable to pray as often as my tradition bids me to: It is hard to fit into a busy schedule; other obligations vie for my attention; I do not always find myself in an environment conducive to prayer. True, these are understandable reasons—but are they *good* reasons? Might our search for the missing Torah be aided by recovering more opportunities to commune with God?

Even as we regain a part of our tradition through the mitzvah of prayer, we also have a chance to add to it by exploring new and different *forms* of prayer. Especially during individual *tefillah* (prayer), we might include selections of modern poetry or blessings we have composed ourselves. We might try various methods of meditation.[18] We can engage in daily study of a sacred text as an act of personal devotion. The abundance of creative liturgy today enables us to discover fascinating ways of combining traditional prayers with newer expressions.

Kashrut. As time goes on, more and more Reform Jews seem to be rediscovering the link between who we are and what we eat (or refrain

---

17: See, for example, Chaim Stern, ed., *On the Doorposts of Your House* (New York: Central Conference of American Rabbis, 1994), 27f.

18: Among the many excellent books on Jewish meditation, I especially recommend the following: Aryeh Kaplan's *Jewish Meditation* (New York: Schocken Books, 1985) provides a good historical and conceptual treatment of the subject. Several meditation exercises can be found in Steven A. Fisdel, *The Practice of Kabbalah* (Northvale, NJ: Jason Aronson, 1996).

from eating). Since *kashrut*, for liberal Jews, does not have to be an all-or-nothing affair, our observance ranges from abstaining from *chametz* on Pesach, to removing certain animals from our diet, all the way to the detailed regulations in the *Shulchan Aruch*. Here, again, the quest for the hidden Torah opens up the possibility of new observance heretofore not associated with traditional *kashrut*. For moral, ecological reasons, many Jews will no longer consume the flesh of any mammal. Others have developed the notion of "eco-*kashrut*," claiming that the natural evolution of the biblical dietary laws should lead us to a strictly vegetarian diet.[19] These paths, too, are open for our exploration.

Poverty and homelessness. Our quest takes us from ritual into the realm of social action. We all know that children go to bed hungry in the Third World and in our own neighborhoods. We also know that we now have the technological capability to produce enough food from the earth to feed every human being on the planet. But, of course, there are reasons why we have not yet gotten around to doing so. There are economic and geopolitical factors to consider, uneven distribution of resources and population, and so on. Yet if we *really believed* that our inertia becomes a screen to block out the light of the hidden Torah, and that we shall never achieve completeness for our world—or for ourselves—until that screen is removed, would we become more motivated to act? There is a modern Hebrew expression for someone passionately obsessed about an issue: *meshugah ba-davar*. This literally means "crazy about the thing." We normally consider crazy people to be simple and naive. Perhaps that is one of the lessons of the hidden Torah: The observance of a mitzvah may be simpler than our rationalizations to evade it.

A Compass for the Journey

There is one further question we must ask. Even if we agree to embark on this quest, how will we know if we have discovered the hidden Written Torah? Since we know how tempting it is to claim divine sanction for our personal agendas, how can we avoid self-delusion?

19: See, for example, Zalman Schachter-Shalomi, *Paradigm Shift* (Northvale, NJ: Jason Aronson, 1993), 269f; also Arthur Green, *Seek My Face, Speak My Name* (Northvale, NJ: Jason Aronson, 1992), 87f.

Although the final outcome cannot be determined with absolute certainty, I believe that we do have a compass to guide us on our way, derived from the literary imagery in the Zohar passage cited above. The recovery of the first set of tablets, which the Zohar compares to the union of Ruth and Boaz, results in a sense of reintegration and harmony. Likewise, in those moments when the performance of mitzvot apprehends letters from the primordial tablets and draws them back into the world, they will fill in a blank space of our present Oral Torah and bestow upon us a sense of wholeness.

This reintegration will take place on three levels. First, on a global scale, the kabbalist Rabbi Yitzchak Luria taught that our efforts toward *tikkun olam* (the mending of the world) will cause the fragmented sparks of the Divine Presence to reunite and make us at one with the earth, with one another, and with God. Second, the reintegration will take place within the Jewish people; when we regain the Written Torah, we regain it not only for one movement but for all Jews. If our quest is successful, dare we hope that our discoveries may even mend the rifts in *klal Yisrael* and bind us into one united people?

Third, this sense of wholeness will be experienced within the self. A hasidic story will serve to illustrate the dilemma we face. There was once a man so absentminded that he could not leave the house without forgetting something. Either he neglected to brush his teeth, or his socks were mismatched, or he completely forgot where he was supposed to go. After a long period of frustration, his wife came upon an idea. "Tomorrow morning," she said, "I will leave a list pinned onto the bedpost. When you wake up, just follow everything in order." The next morning, as the man came downstairs into the kitchen, his wife greeted him with a friendly smile. "Did the list help?" she asked. "Well, almost," he replied. "Here is my tie, here are my shoes, here is my briefcase—but where am I?"

We live in a world that is so diverse, and we define ourselves in so many ways, that we often wonder where our real identity resides. Like the shattered tablets, each of us is divided into multiple, fragmented identities. There is the piece of our profession, which tells something about ourselves but by no means all. There is the piece of nationality, which defines us in a different way. Then there are the shards of culture: socioeconomic class, hobbies, and sexual identity, each capturing another portion of our identity. But every once in a while we stop chasing after these multiple selves long enough to ponder: Where am I?

The process of "finding oneself" cannot be achieved without the discovery of where one belongs. Our tradition teaches that, since every Jewish soul was present at Mount Sinai when Torah was revealed, every Jew belongs to the historical family of the Jewish people. In our communal search to bring the hidden Written Torah into our world, we may discover that its letters will serve as the cement to bind together the fragments of our multiple identities. By assembling these holy letters into a Torah rediscovered, the Jewish people will play its collective role in the completion of our world.

Beyond Autonomy and Authority: The New Dilemma of Liberal Judaism

MICHAEL L. MORGAN

In the 1950s and 1960s, in postwar American culture and society, the most dreaded vices were conformity and alienation. Our greatest fears were immersion into an impersonal mass in which decisions were made for us and detachment from our choices and our very selves. Together these twin features characterized the antiheroes of numerous films and books, those lost in a commodified, bureaucratized, and indulgent society. Such antiheroes were drowned in the lonely crowd of a vast consumer society; they were the organization men, the homogenized, or the "new philistines," as Hannah Arendt called them.

There were two great themes in liberal Jewish theology in America in those days. The one arose from the threat of materialism and the need for a transcendent ground of meaning and purpose. This was the problem of faith: What is it, and how is it possible in the modern, industrial, scientific world? The second was more closely tied to the twin vices cited above; it was the problem of autonomy, or self-determination, and authority. If human existence is characterized by freedom and self-determination, how can authentic Jews be bound to authorities external to the self—to the past, to tradition, to the community, and ultimately to God? Does not life in the religious world stifle and threaten to annihilate one's individuality and indeed one's selfhood? If modernity involves autonomy and self-determination, then how can one be genuinely Jewish and a modern person both at once?

In the postwar period, all the major American Jewish thinkers, young and old, articulated this theme in one way or another. All struggled to understand how modern Jews could submit to the authority of *halachah* and still be free human agents. All worried about the tension between autonomy and authority in Judaism.

The intellectual origins of this problem for liberal religion in the West go back at least to Baruch Spinoza in the seventeenth century, but there is reason to treat the great German philosopher Immanuel Kant as its foremost and most influential proponent. In the 1780s Kant developed his critical philosophy. In it he analyzed everyday and scientific knowledge, restricted the scope of metaphysics and our knowledge of God, the soul, and human freedom, and then set out to locate human agency and morality as a further dimension of human existence; being human involved not only knowledge of nature but also action in the world. Here he found the core of our humanity, for human agency was grounded in a number of factors, among them freedom, the highest expression of which was autonomy. Kant inherited from the Stoics the distinction between internal and external influences on the self. Autonomy and reason constituted the internal influences on the self and hence the self's real nature. Passion and desire were external to this true self and involved reactions to threats, enticements, and other external factors. Morality was a matter of becoming increasingly internal, honest to one's internal and truest self. That is, it was to become increasingly rational and autonomous, free and independent. Allowing oneself to be moved by external factors—fear, jealousy, hatred, love, and such emotions—was to be heteronomous and alienated from one's genuine self. In short, for Kant, autonomy and authority were utterly opposed. Unless the dictates of a religious way of life could be made autonomous, unless they could be integrated into the self and their otherness neutralized, traditional religion would have to be relegated to the unauthentic.

The Kantian legacy of this problem weighed heavily on the minds of Jewish theologians in the period following World War II. Article after article, by Jacob Petuchowski, Alvin Reines, Eugene Borowitz, Emil Fackenheim, and many others, formulated the problem along broadly Kantian lines—now extended by existential thought—and tried to solve it. Perhaps no better account of the problem and its solution can be found than in Emil Fackenheim's essays, especially "The Dilemma of Liberal Judaism" and "Revealed Morality and Kantian Thought." Both essays are reprinted in *Quest for Past and Future* (1968), but they appeared earlier in the sixties. In the Kant essay, Fackenheim sets out Kant's position as we find it in the *Groundwork for a Metaphysic of Morals*, with the sharp distinction between autonomous and heteronomous imperatives. As Fackenheim sees it, if Kant is right and all morality is essentially autonomous, then no heteronomous or divinely commanded set of imperatives can be moral. Hence, if Kant is right, there simply is no such thing as a "revealed morality." If liberal Judaism is to survive in any serious sense, Kant must be wrong.

In the "Dilemma" essay, Fackenheim's scope is broader but his focus is the same. How can Judaism be both Jewish and liberal? For liberalism focuses on the individual, on the present, and on the human, whereas Judaism gives priority to the community over the individual, to the past over the present, and to God over man. And the reason for these tensions is that for modern man the essence of selfhood is freedom or autonomy. The more genuine moderns become, the more their opposition to traditional Judaism. This is the dilemma of liberal Judaism.

It is not clear that there ever was offered a completely satisfactory solution to this dilemma or problem, formulated this way. If there ever was a solution worth taking seriously, it was that built on the work of Martin Buber and Franz Rosenzweig. Indeed, if one were to reread the most fruitful essays of the period, one would find that they often call upon Buber and Rosenzweig as their guides. The key to the Buber–Rosenzweig solution, as I shall call it, was to focus on revelation and, by rethinking the concept of revelation, to locate the ways in which divine power and human freedom coexist. Broadly speaking, the solution involved appreciating that revelation was an event, not a literal proposition, and that both within that event and after it, there was present both Divine Presence and human receptivity. In short, both within the event of revelation itself and after that event, in the responsiveness to it, there is an element of divine mandate—what Fackenheim often called God's "singling out"—and an element of human receptivity, openness and then interpretation. To be sure, Buber and Rosenzweig differed on important features of their accounts, certainly regarding the context for the event and the role of religious law, but fundamentally they agreed that revelation included both divine or heteronomous and human or autonomous dimensions. As Buber put it, in the moment of revelation, you feel both that you are being summoned and that everything is up to you.

All of this was very important to liberal or Reform Judaism in the postwar period. Ideologically, Reform Judaism was largely still committed to some notion of classical Reform. There was a minimizing of ritual, an emphasis on universality, and priority on ethics. Hence, for many Reform Jews and their leaders, it was a time ripe to emphasize individual freedom and moral integrity, as long as this could be reconciled with God and some notion of God's underwriting moral principle. Doubtless the Buber–Rosenzweig solution was understood by few and accepted by even fewer, and the issue of the tension between *halachah* and individual freedom was yet to receive attention, although even then there was widespread adherence to the view that for Reform Jews practice was a matter of individual preference and individual choice. Still, the tension between autonomy and authority was critical to liberal Jewish self-understanding.

Given all that I have said, it is not surprising that the problem and the dichotomy loomed so large. From other points of view, however, it is quite surprising. First, for Kant, when one looks carefully, the notion of autonomy or self-determination is a puzzling one. In John Locke and Jean Jacques Rousseau, whose work Kant revered, freedom is connected with rules or law. To be genuinely free is to act according to law; to be genuinely free is to be bound or conditioned. Free, then, means free from the passions, free from external obstacles and coercion, but it does not mean free from all coercion or free from all determination. As long as the determination or direction comes from oneself, then one is free. In the postwar period, of course, free in common parlance meant spontaneous or uncoerced, and there was rarely any attempt made to distinguish between good coercion and bad coercion.

Furthermore, in Kant, as in his predecessors all the way back to the Stoics, freedom was deeply connected with reason and with universality. Freedom meant free from passion and in harmony with reason, insofar as reason was the faculty responsible for those unconditional, universal imperatives that expressed who one really was, what one shared with all rational agents, and what should ground one's character and one's ideal as a human being. In short, to be free for Kant meant to be rational. Hence, the issue for him was the tension between reason, on the one hand, and tradition, community, solidarity, and fidelity, on the other. By the postwar period, of course, we were long past the debate over the role of reason and rationality in human existence. Most of us were certainly willing to accept the importance—some even the priority—of nonrational factors in human personality. After Nazism and fascism, there were many who wanted a return to reason as a safeguard against rampant irrationalism, and even some who worried about the kind of reason one should affirm, since instrumental rationality had served Nazi ends just as efficiently as other ends. But in America there was a sense that the issue of reason and the nonrational was clear.

Finally, ever since Hobbes, Locke, and the contract tradition, modern political thinkers had realized that there were a variety of ways of reconciling freedom and authority, or at least individual freedom and political authority. In a sense, after the seventeenth century, there was no longer a problem of authority and autonomy. Autonomy was basic, but one could derive legitimate authority from it. In the postwar period, everyone knew this, but it seemed to have virtually no effect on the debate about liberal Judaism. And the reason is obvious: A political society might be usefully conceived as constructed by free agents for certain purposes, but the society of God with human beings, the Jewish people, could not, at least in the fundamental sense. The people of Israel was grounded in covenant all right, but the covenant was not between human participants; it was between God and the Jews. How that covenant involved both divine mandate and human freedom was another matter.

The dilemma of liberal Judaism as the tension between autonomy and authority, then, arises out of modernity and the tradition of the Enlightenment, and it has persevered for us, although modified, because it has seemed to articulate certain aspects of our problematic situation as Jews living in a Western democratic society. The dilemma rests on a dichotomy between free and controlled, between self-determination and other-determination. It harbors a conception of the ideal self as sharing a deep harmony with other rational selves and of society as built up out of individual building blocks that either collaborate with or impede one another's actions and projects. The general good is a collection of all the goods we share and the means we need to facilitate their acquisition.

As we turn from the postwar period to our own day and turn from its culture and ideas to our own, it is, I think, inappropriate and troubling to persist in applying this dichotomy to our own situation. This old dilemma is not our dilemma. As Jews living in the final moments of the twentieth century, too much has occurred, culturally, intellectually, socially, and historically, to allow us to adopt this formulation as compelling and appropriate for us. Our task is not the same task as the one that faced our intellectual leaders of the postwar period. Their dilemma depended upon certain ways of understanding human existence and human community; it depended upon a dichotomy that in turn expressed a certain view of the human condition. Much of this intellectual infrastructure can no longer be accepted. It is not that we now have new solutions to the old dilemma; it is that the old dilemma should no longer make sense to us. It may be that there is a new dilemma to replace the old, but the way to see that is to recognize first why the old one is no longer appropriate for us.

In the 1960s and then with increasing prominence, there emerged a view of human selfhood and human agency that now seems compelling. Its roots go far back into the Western tradition, to Montaigne, Vico, Hegel, and then to developments in hermeneutics and existentialism in our own century. It is a biblical view too, rooted in the narrative character of the biblical experience. The view is a view of who we are as human beings and how our lives are bound up with community, tradition, history, and identity. Within this view, I believe, the old dichotomy of autonomy and authority no long functions as it once did. On the old view, the two were exclusive; when one existed it threatened and ruled out the other. On the new view, all our decisions and all our actions are immersed in both. They are complementary and co-existent. There is no freedom without constraint; our lives regularly involve interpretation and decision within a situation that enables and limits what we understand and what we do. This is the gist of it, but let me now take a moment to explain.

The view that I am trying to identify, of us as historically situated agents, as hermeneutical beings, as self-interpreting animals, grows out of the tradition of German idealism, out of the debates in the late nineteenth century about the differences between the human sciences (the *Geisteswissenschaften*) and the natural sciences, out of the development of existential philosophy and anthropology, and out of the understanding of human existence as hermeneutical, that is, interpretive. The result is a conception of us as interpreting and acting human beings, immersed at any given moment in a specific historical situation, shaped and enabled by the resources of that situation—its language, cultural artifacts and practices, social patterns, relationships, and much else. We always think, understand, and choose from the specific point of view that is ours, given our conceptual and emotional resources, our understandings, our expectations, our abilities. This point of view or perspective, this "I," is irreducible. We may, in various ways, try to transcend it, to become impersonal and detached from the peculiarities of our particular personality, but in some way or other we never wholly succeed. To grasp our mode of life is to grasp how we find and adjust the meanings of the world for ourselves.

Let me suggest an image of this conception. It has been used by others, by Ronald Dworkin for example, who used it to portray the way in which the Supreme Court engages in constitutional interpretation. The image is this: When we are born and begin to grow and develop, we enter a complex network of stories, a novel with many chapters, some strung out in serial order, others overlapping in various ways. Our task in part is to write our chapter or chapters as part of this network, of this existing novel. The existing chapters were written by others still living and many who are no longer living. Some parts of these materials we read and digest, but not all. Still, while our task is to write our story into the fabric of this novel, we are free to create and yet constrained by what has already been written, by the language we inherit, by characters already introduced, by events already narrated and perhaps recalled, and by much else. Our chapter, then, will express our narration of how the story goes, and this means that it is a part of the total story told from our special point of view, with our way of understanding events and people, our attitude toward issues and conduct, our interests, hopes, and desires. Furthermore, it will express our creativity, but it is not unconditional creativity. Since we are writing part of an existing novel, there are limits on how our story will go, no matter how creative we are. The limits we choose are in a sense grounded in our creativity, but there are also limits that we do not choose, ones that give shape, direction, possibility to our narrative, and without which we could not write at all.

Let us call this view of human existence "historically situated agency." Others might call it a view of the "narrative self" or the "hermeneutical or interpretive self." Whatever we call it, the view has a powerful grip on many today, and I would like to suggest that it captures in a fuller and more accurate way how we live than did the old view of us as rational agents with desires, some common to all, some peculiar to us. There is an excellent picture of the contrast between the older universal self and the new situated self in chapter 2 of Sartre's *Anti-Semite and Jew*, but the best recent accounts I know of are in the work of Charles Taylor, such as *Sources of the Self*, and in Michael

Sandel's *Justice and the Limits of Liberalism* and *Democracy and Its Discontents*.

This view of the human condition is not a parochial or idiosyncratic one. It has arisen and should arise for us as Jews from three contemporary sources. As I indicated, there are antecedents—from Kant and Hegel to Nietzsche, Dilthey, Heidegger, and Gadamer. And three recent events collectively encourage this view. One is a cluster of intellectual developments that focus away from disengaged thinking and toward the historically situated agent. These developments flourished in the 1970s and early 1980s. The leading proponents are Thomas Kuhn, Clifford Geertz, Richard Rorty, Alasdair MacIntyre, Michael Sandel, and Charles Taylor. Their legacy is a conviction that domain after domain of our lives must be understood in terms of history, tradition, and community.

The second event is the turn in American culture from a pervasive universalism to a rich sense of particular rootedness. Already in the 1960s but certainly in the 1970s, there were stronger and stronger tendencies toward ethnic, religious, cultural, and interest-based affiliations and connectedness. This movement was and continues to be part of a greater appreciation for the values and meanings constituted by people's associations, practices, memories, and more. At its core is the notion of the historically situated, communally constituted self.

Finally, for Jews the emphasis on historical context and historicity arose as the central issue of post-Holocaust Jewish thought. By this we mean that set of reflections on the meaning of the *Shoah* for Judaism today, which began in the 1960s and extended into the 1980s, as exemplified best in the work of Emil Fackenheim. Here the complex interplay between Jewish belief and practice, on the one hand, and historical situation, on the other, became the guiding matrix for any responsible post-Holocaust Judaism. And the conception of the self and of human existence that lies behind that teaching is the one we have identified, that of the self as a historically situated agent. The Holocaust may have stimulated no new conception of God, Israel, or the covenant, but it did stimulate the notion of the historically situated Jewish self who must face the threat of annihilation honestly and nonetheless persevere as a Jew. No detached point of view is possible for post-Holocaust Jews; history requires that our point of view forever be from this side of the abyss.

Let us take stock. Today a host of factors recommend a view of human selfhood and the human condition as a historically situated agency. It is a view that breaks with the older view of the self as a nucleus of universally shared abilities, attitudes, and desires and of thinking and acting as ideally conducted from a detached, impersonal, ahistorical perspective. Yet it was this older view that supported the Kantian, let us call it, picture of authority and autonomy and the old dilemma of how to reconcile, in Judaism, individual self-determination with the authority of tradition, law, and ultimately God. If the old view is jettisoned, then the old dilemma dissolves. And we can see this in fact and not merely in principle. In the old view, autonomy and authority were exclusive; the more of one, the less of the other. In the new view, every decision, every act of interpretation, and every action is characterized by both constraints and creativity. Every interpretation is conducted within a set of givens, of a language, of background meanings, and of interests, et cetera. We are always writing a new story with old resources. A wholly new narrative is utterly impossible, and even an exact replication is the outcome of *our* act of replication. The cooperation of external limitation with internal spontaneity is unavoidable. Authority and autonomy are not a problem of irreconcilables; they are a conjunction of undeniables.

In one sense, then, the old dilemma is dissolved. It no longer exists for us as it once did. We should deny it the central place we so often give it in our debates and in our self-understanding. Reform or liberal Judaism is not a Judaism that chooses autonomy over authority. All genuine modern Judaisms are liberal and Jewish. They must be both. The issue is not whether to be both but how to be both.

But perhaps this conclusion is too glib. It certainly is too sanguine, for it makes it sound as if a great burden has been shifted and a great weight lifted. In fact, if it accomplishes anything, this conclusion should refocus our attention. It should make us attentive to those new issues that arise when we understand our situation as I have suggested. These issues can, like the old situation, be understood as a dilemma.

The view of human agency as historically situated might seem to have a very negative feature. That feature is often associated with relativism and especially moral relativism. In general, many of us might find it appalling to reduce moral principle to historical or cultural or communal contexts. On the conception we have recommended, such values are either given as part of a community's or tradition's resources and hence can be accepted or rejected, or they arise for an individual or community in opposition to what is received. In either case, however, the values or principles are relative and temporary. Hence the dilemma: If we accept historically situated agency, we must give up absolute values; if we accept absolute values, we must give up historically situated agency. And indeed the reality of Auschwitz and of so much violence and cruelty and atrocity in our world makes the latter option seem much the wiser.

If this is the new dilemma of liberal Judaism, it is a dilemma because we want to understand ourselves properly as human beings and still be liberal Jews. Its point can be put somewhat differently: If indeed we are historically situated agents, must we give up standards of right and wrong that we consider unimpeachable and deeply abiding? Do we have to admit that there is no cruelty, no atrocity, no suffering that simply must be opposed, under all foreseeable conditions? Can we, embedded in history, not also be advocates of principle?

This problem, I propose, is the new dilemma of liberal Judaism. If we are all interpretive and historical beings, from where does the firmness, the solidity of our principles come? Once that firmness was found in God or in Nature or in Beauty or in Reason. One of these sources was the ground of objectivity for our values and our sense of the right, the good, the object of aspiration and integrity and respect. Where is that ground today? Is there a dilemma that requires us to choose one horn or the other? Or can we locate a new source for ourselves?

This question, central to our task, points to another worry. It might be thought that I have set aside with too much facility the old dichotomy of autonomy and authority. After all, one might argue, there still must be a difference between acting under authority and acting out of self-determination. Simply changing our conception of human agency does not change the fact that we want to distinguish between doing something because we are told to do so by an authoritative official and doing so because we want to and choose to do so for ourselves. In short, just as we still want to have some understanding of objectivity and the firmness of principles, so we still want some understanding of the distinction between authority and autonomy, of acting on our own and acting because we are bound to.

In both cases, I think, we can retain some of the old notions but show why and how they must be altered, given our changed understanding of who we are and how we act. Let us begin with acting autonomously and on authority. Since we now appreciate that in a deep sense all our conduct is grounded both in what we contribute and in what is given to us, the everyday distinction between autonomous and authoritative conduct must be reinterpreted in terms of what kinds of factors are most relevant and what role these factors play. Take Sabbath observance. We are inclined to think that the more traditional behavior is grounded in authority—that the more its style matches that of Orthodoxy—the more authoritative the practice, and so on. We also tend to think that when people express a sense of undeniability, of having to perform certain acts, of never questioning them, of actions performed according to binding rules, and so forth, this means the acts are done on authority. On the other hand, when they are done by Reform Jews, whose style is different and who may have not done them often before, who we think of as having chosen to do them for personal reasons, we think of the acts—often the very same acts—as done autonomously. Hence, we do have an everyday way of distinguishing these acts, but the criteria we use are a cluster of features that we associate with one pole or the other.

Something similar is true, I believe, with regard to the new dilemma, about the firmness of our standards given our newly appreciated historical condition. Objectivity, firmness, and such notions are not to be understood without some attention to context. They are terms or notions defined by context. Once we associated them with some standards or credentials such as "commanded by God" or "rational" or "grounded in Nature," but these credentials no longer work for most of us. To be sure, we still mean something firm and reliable and as stable as possible by notions like truth, right, goodness, and such. But in practice the principles that we hold to be right—e.g., that cruelty and atrocity are horrible and always to be utterly opposed, chastised, and punished—are determined not by satisfying such principles. Rather they are the ones that we hold with utter conviction, that we are unwilling to abandon no matter what, that are normally staples of the traditions to which we are loyal, and that are the principles of the community or communities to which we feel the greatest sense of solidarity. One way of putting this, I believe, is to say that these principles are objective and that principles that meet these credentials are absolute. Indeed, given who we are and the kind of beings we are, one might wonder what else it might mean for a principle to be absolute or unconditional. We could be wrong, but we do not think we are. And one day we might change our minds, but now we do not think that we will.

You might worry, by now, that the views I have been expressing are so deeply incompatible with Judaism as we understand it that no matter how compelling, we certainly should reject them and return to the absolute values of a divinely commanded tradition and leave history behind. They are not, but this is not the time, of course, to discuss this critical issue fully. It raises the question, What is Judaism traditionally, if not Jewish texts, ideas, and other evidence of Jewish life and practice and belief, as we now interpret it, from our own particular points of view? It also raises the question whether Jews and Jewish thinkers have not always viewed their Judaism as something interpreted and articulated by their leaders, their thinkers, and their communities at different times in different ways with differing resources. In short, it might very well be that the view I have recommended, which argues that the vocabulary of autonomy and authority should not be the vocabulary for discussing the nature of liberal Judaism today, is fully compatible with Judaism as it traditionally has seen itself and as we now must see it. Judaism is and has been not simply God-given and transcendent. God created not religion but the world; Judaism is the result of a dialogue between heaven and earth, a dialogue that cannot do without the contributions of both. That insight is the key to understanding and solving the new dilemma of liberal Judaism.

Mitzvah and Autonomy

HERBERT BRONSTEIN

The prayer recited immediately before the central affirmation of Jewish faith-identity (the *Shema*) has since early rabbinic times been called the "love prayer" (*ahavah*). In this prayer, the emphasis is on Torah and mitzvot, teaching and commandment. God's love for Israel is expressed in the gift of divine teaching and commandment as a way that will lead to blessing. Israel's love and devotion to God are realized by immersion in Torah, the teaching, and in loyal response to the divine imperative lived out in actual deeds, mitzvot.

No one knowledgeable about Judaism will deny that these terms, *Torah* and *mitzvah*, are central to its lexicon. They are integral with the overarching metaphor of the relationship between God and the community of Israel: the covenant (*b'rit*). No metaphor for the relationship between God and the people of Israel has been more pervasive in the Jewish religious outlook. This has been the case from the stories of the ancestors, through the prophetic literature, the later codes of law, and rabbinic discourse, to the theological expositions of our own day. The covenant relationship, whether conceived of as partnership, alliance, or bond with God, or as engagement with God, can be actualized on the human side only through mitzvot, that is, deeds, actions, observances, practices.

This interrelated cluster of terms (*Torah, mitzvah, b'rit*) implies a spiritual mindset that assumes an authority that transcends the individual ego, a sense of obligation, an "ought" to an Other beyond the individual self. Furthermore, after Sinai, the covenant with God is with the entire community of Israel as a group. All of these constructs—Torah, mitzvah, *b'rit*—therefore imply not only a strong sense of obligation to God but also a communal consciousness, a sense of "we" that transcends the "me" or ego. This is clearly manifest in the communal stance of Jewish worship, of communal Jewish confession, of communal moral obligation, all of which have long been recognized as characteristics of historic Jewish identity.

Yet, the very opposite of this Judaic mindset has risen to the position of a central credo, if not defining mark, of Reform Judaism: the principle of autonomy. Today, this principle is understood widely among most Reform Jews simply to mean personal choice in matters of religious observance. In addition, autonomy has increasingly become a litmus test for Reform Jewish doctrinal acceptability. The general view is that if one is a Reform Jew, one accepts the idea of personal choice in religious matters. "Autonomy," like "pluralism" with which it is often linked (although they are not identical),[1] is by now stated as a "given" of Reform Judaism to the extent that while little else is authoritative in Reform Judaism, without at least lip service to the authority of this one doctrine, someone might be considered "outside the pale."

At the same time, there is also widespread unease with the tension and even contradiction between autonomy on the one side and, on the other side, the historic sense of obligation (*chovah*) to a transcendent authority beyond the self and its individual choices. This tension is reflected in the opening address of Eric Yoffie, as president-elect of the Union of American Hebrew Congregations (Atlanta, 1995). "My goal," he says, "is a movement that is thoroughly Reform." This is followed by an explanation of what "Reform" means, a kind of definition: "grounded in the principles of autonomy and pluralism." At the same time, Rabbi Yoffie balances this with the following words: "a movement also willing to talk of obligations, to call for observance that is regular and consistent, and to assert that our actions need not always begin with our own impulses." In this latter sentence, though the word *authority* is not used, nevertheless at least some degree of authority is certainly implied. Then, in another finely balanced sentence, Rabbi Yoffie also speaks of another contribution of Reform to Judaism, "a movement that does not see Torah as the immutable word of God." Yet, a new call to action, certainly evoked by the conditions of our

---

1: A pluralistic outlook would respect and allow for both: voices of Judaism in which personal autonomy is central and views in which the authority of tradition is decisive.

time, is expressed in the words: "At the same time [Reform Judaism must be a movement] that sees the renewal of Torah as the only route to the renewal of the Jewish people."

While autonomy is continually invoked as a defining mark of Reform Judaism, there has been little thought and less analysis given to the origins of the association of Reform Judaism with autonomy. The implications and limitations of autonomy as doctrine for any form of Judaism need to be considered, as does the question of whether such a religious credo is salutary for spirituality in general, or even for human well-being in our time. Few, even in recent years, aside from Eugene Borowitz, the Jewish theologian who has probed this issue most thoroughly on the basis of broad knowledge and deep personal absorption in it, have endeavored to resolve the problem of the validity and viability of autonomy in principle and practice.[2]

Borowitz is well aware of the breakdown of the intellectual constructs that have formed the "Faith of Modernity," of which autonomy is an integral part, such as the belief that there would be inevitable progress in the conditions of human well-being in every sense through reason and science, a belief he himself calls "secular messianism." He is well aware of the dangers of rampant anarchic individualism to human well-being everywhere.

Borowitz shifts the center of his theology from an emphasis on Judaism as a universal system of morals for all humankind (the idea of the Jew as equivalent to being a good human being) to the distinctively Jewish self, a self bound in a particular unique Jewish covenant with God. He endeavors to resolve the tension between the sense of obligation characteristic of Judaism and personal choice by evoking the needs and aspirations of the Jewish people, the Jewish community, its purposes and continuity. With this in mind, he asserts that his theological "move" is essentially "post-modern." Despite this, he ultimately comes down to the bottom-line primacy of personal autonomy: "For even in the post-modern vision of covenant with its strongly contextualized view of personal individuality, each Jewish self ultimately stands alone before God" (*Choices in Modern Jewish Thought*, 310).

We have to ask whether any system of thought can be called post-

---

2: For the views of Dr. Borowitz on autonomy, see *Choices in Modern Jewish Thought* (New York: Behrman House, 1983, 1995); *Renewing the Covenant* (Philadelphia: Jewish Publication Society of America, 1991).

modern that gives such pride of place to a principle or construct so integral to the other elements of modernity, such as the belief in universal progress through reason. Thinkers as diverse as Charles P. Taylor (*The Sources of the Self,* 1989), Roger Shattuck (*Forbidden Knowledge,* 1996) and, more popularly, John Ralston Saul (*Voltaire's Bastards,* 1992) have all demonstrated the connection between the ideas clustered around personal autonomy and a continued emphasis on the self, its prerogatives and its rights. "Overemphasis on personal individual autonomy, according to these thinkers, has contributed to a diminution of a sense of community, the atrophy of regard for other human beings, and moral relativism. These together threaten us, for example, with violence and environmental deterioration."

Why should we be afraid to subject autonomy as a religious doctrine to as thorough a critique as Reform Jews pride themselves on applying to any other doctrine? Why not consider it in balance with other religious values such as Jewish communal identity, which might impose upon personal autonomy limitations beneficial to the community and perhaps to personal religious growth as well? Further, should not the issues of autonomy and authority discussed thus far among rabbis and academicians be brought out of the academy into wider popular discourse among laypeople whom we are increasingly involving in decisions about Jewish worship and Jewish religious observance?

Especially because we have seen autonomy asserted as so axiomatic for Reform Judaism as to be beyond discussion, the time is ripe for us to examine the principle of autonomy in a religious context. Assuming nothing, we can take a fresh look at its validity and its effect on our everyday religious life and on the continuity of the Jewish people as a religious community whose core is Torah, our religious heritage known and lived.

As to whether autonomy is a doctrine salutary for Judaism, for religion, or for human well-being, a positive answer can be given *only if we understand autonomy as a choice against idols,* as I shall endeavor to show before proceeding to practical directions. But first, we must consider the loss of a sense of obligation in Reform Judaism and the intellectual credibility of autonomy as creed.

Obligation and Authority

In all traditional societies, however else the "self" was conceived, it was constituted by a web of relationships imbedded in the ongoing life of a community. The "self" was also considered to be in some way a part of, or related to, a transcendent wholeness beyond it, whether a world-soul or a web of life or a life process. Scripture speaks of the human being as a creature of God made in the image of God. Self-fulfillment in all primordial religious traditions is realized by identification of the individual self with some purpose or reality beyond the self. In our time, Charles Taylor describes in *The Sources of the Self* how the individual self, in contrast, is seen as constituted by a cluster of individual rights and privileges. Self-fulfillment is now viewed as fulfillment through one's own individual preferential pursuits. The pride of place occupied by autonomy as personal choice reflects this contemporary concept of the self. It is a view of the self that stands in opposition to the sense of religious obligation (*chovah*) taught by classical Judaism. Reform Jews and their leaders have been particularly wary of such words as *obligation*, *ought*, and *requirement*. Many a Reform Jew who is perturbed by the notion that Reform Judaism might teach any table of requirements based on religious obligation will be surprised to learn that the doctrine of autonomy initially came into liberal Jewish thinking heavily weighted with a sense of obligation to a law that is universal and beyond the self. While we still assert our autonomy, we have lost that sense of obligation. The philosopher associated with a systematic exposition of the idea of autonomy, the one who had the most influence on the mentality of the exponents of Reform Judaism, was Immanuel Kant (1724–1804). In an essay (1784) entitled "What Is the Enlightenment?" (*Aufklarung*), Kant responded to ridicule by enemies of the Enlightenment as *"aufklarei"* by admirably articulating its essence as a morally principled movement at the very core of which was the struggle against the oppressive rule or "tutelage" of others, particularly institutions and power structures, over our own individual thoughts, wills, and action. Kant called that oppressive domination by others over our individual integrity "heteronomy." This motif, especially because of the totalitarianism of our century and the ongoing struggle for freedom and human rights, still resonates strongly with us. It is a position formative of the American ethos of individual freedom. For most of us it means, simply, standing up for what we believe.

It had even more meaning for Jews of Western and Central Europe during the movement to emancipate them from civil disabilities, a process that was itself a result of the intellectual movement of the Enlightenment, which preached reason and tolerance. European Jews could be particularly enthusiastic about a clarion call to autonomy, bound up with their own emancipation into the civil, social, and economic order.

Further, in the thinking of Kant, there was a strong link between reason, autonomy and morality. This linkage was at the very core of what the Enlightenment called "civilization." Progress was inevitable because reason would redeem the world from all ills. And this is exactly what early Reform Jewish advocates saw as the core of Judaism itself![3] They could present Judaism to societies that hardly knew Jews and only gradually accepted them, as among the most rational, enlightened, and moral of all religions and therefore worthy of a place in progressive Western society. It is no wonder that educated German Jews taught Kant to their children as if it were catechism.[4]

This brings us to the element of obligation. We must recall that, for Kant, autonomy was linked with the premise that through reason the individual person would discover a moral law applicable everywhere and equally to the behavior of all people. To the authority of that universal moral law, once realized, the individual in turn becomes morally subject.[5] In Kant, as in early Reform Judaism, autonomy and morality in the religious sense were linked indissolubly to a strong sense of obligation.

How different the situation is today! Our people do not live in an overly repressive, morally forbidding, or socially restrictive culture. On the contrary, our culture is one in which participants boast about decadent behavior. In the most sensationally prurient "wash your dirty linen in public" television talk shows, many regularly and passionately defend the most outrageous behavior, hurtful not only to others but to

---

3: Among them, Abraham Geiger and his successors in nineteenth-century Germany, and David Einhorn and Isaac Mayer Wise and their successors in late nineteenth-century America.

4: Personal correspondence with Paul Mendes-Flohr.

5: H.J. Paton, *The Moral Law or Groundwork of the Metaphysics of Morals* (London, 1950), chap. 2.

the participants themselves, with a sententiously proclaimed dictum that seems to quell all and every objection: "This is my personal choice, you do what you want, I do what I want, and who is to judge me?" We must at least consider this cultural context whenever we assert the primacy of the individual self as an overarching decisive element in Reform Jewish teaching, particularly at a time when the sense of obligation, ought, and duty are in considerable decline.

Nor is it at all strange that the word *freedom* has been absorbed into the religious language and mentality of American Jews. It is customary among Jews today to speak of both Chanukah and Passover as "festivals of freedom". Freedom, is, after all, the emblematic blazon of the United States. But the scriptural text does not say, "Let my people go that they may be free," but rather, "Let my people go that they may serve me." The divine call is not to freedom per se but away from servitude to Pharaoh (a god) to the service of God. This may very well be the key to a truly authentic, indigenous Judaic notion of autonomy.

The service of God necessarily implies a sense of "ought," obligation, and duties. But the word *freedom*, in the sense derived from Enlightenment thought—liberation from any outward obligation—is far more evident in the Reform *Gates of Prayer* than the words *obligation* or *duty* in relation to Torah and mitzvot or covenant.[6]

I sometimes like to say that if a scholar of religions from outer space, i.e., one without bias or preconceptions, were sent to the planet Earth to describe Judaism, he would have to conclude that it is halachically structured, that is, a body of practices that constitute a "way of living." Indeed the Hebrew word *halachah* means "way" or "path." But *halachah* is a word that is quite foreign to liberal Judaism, and to some spokespersons of Reform it is anathema. No doubt this is because Orthodoxy has seized and occupied both the word and concept *halachah* and turned it into an often static and sometimes oppressive religious regime. Once I suggested that the new Reform *Rabbi's Manual* be entitled *halichot,* meaning "pathways." An older rabbi reacted in sheer dismay, "It sounds too much like *halachah,*" he said, and that, he implied, would have been totally out of the question. But should we be disturbed with the metaphor "path" or "way"? We see nothing objection-

---

6: Now at the end of the twentieth century, many Western intellectuals are more likely to believe that the exaltation of personal freedom as the ultimate value cut loose from any other values is likely to eventuate in behavior destructive to others and transformable to evil.

able in the fact that adherents of Hinduism call their religion *Dharma,* "Way." And though Buddhism is a remarkable thought system, the founder began his foundational message at Benares, not with his theoretical formulations on the nature of existence or our experience of existence, but with specific authoritative directions: the "Eightfold Path" with which the seeker is taught to align himself/herself to achieve Nirvana. Islam also speaks of religion not only as *Islam* (total self-commitment) but also *Al-Din* (the actual body of deeds and practices that constitute the religious life). The rational, socially focused aspect of Chinese religion and its highly individualistic mystical manifestation both speak of the Tao, "the Path."

Many today, hungry for a way of life, are seeking a way among these spiritualities. Their teachers do not say to them as we in Reform Judaism have been apt to do, "You might like to choose this option or that; you might find this worthwhile, et cetera." We tend to adhere to the notion that autonomy transcends all and that we must leave people to their own devices. Even in some of our most practical guidebooks, rather than speaking of covenantal commitment or of labor toward a higher purpose or of what is required of Jews, we speak instead of personal benefits that might accrue to the individual. Thus we feed the very narcissism and emphasis on personal satisfaction that so drains our common life of coherence and the individual soul of a purpose beyond the self.

Many years ago I said that the situation of many Reform Jews in the face of our Reform rabbinic refusal to give our people the guidance they are seeking is very similar to the *New Yorker* cartoon in which a nursery-school child looks up at her teacher and says, "Do I have to do today whatever I want to do?" This is very much related to the move among some Reform rabbis away from the rabbi as *moreh derech,* a "teacher of a way," to (in "sociologese") rabbi as "facilitator."

Intellectual Credibility

Reform Judaism's response to modernity was fully to embrace it. One crucial aspect of modernity is the scientific approach, which endeavors to establish factual verity about the material dimension of existence. Through a scientific approach to the study of history and the social life of human beings, we have become aware of social, economic, political, and cultural influences on Judaism over the course of time, influences that affected how Jews lived out their religion in different times and places. We have learned that religious dietary practices, the content and form of our worship, the observance of holidays, the religious status and role of men and women, to give a few examples, have never been static but have changed over the ages. This naturally affects our view of the ongoing authority of religious observances. Now we can apply the same critical methods to such principles as autonomy as a product of history. We can see the cultural causes of its emergence and the original premises behind it and, in this way, test its validity and credibility today.

The prestige of autonomy arose in part from the emphasis in Enlightenment thought on the supreme role of individual reason in making choices. Here we must consider the difference between Kant's view of the power and scope of reason and our own contemporary sense of the limitations of reason. We remember that the nemesis of autonomy was, for Kant, heteronomy, the rule of others, particularly in institutional form, over our thoughts and wills, decisions and actions. For Kant, heteronomy was also the influence of what he called "the sensible" or material world. Today, we call these the influence of "material determinism." Kant, believing that freedom was an attribute of reason, asserted that reason transcended these outside influences. He believed that the autonomous individual was free to discover the moral law and obligate himself to it. To Kant and others before and after him, the conviction that there is a free, transcendent reason that can rise above the pressure and influence of events and material circumstances in which we live was completely tenable. While we too still must and do expect moral choices from people, we know as well that social and cultural conditions, our own emotions, group psychology all affect our thinking, our ideas, our reasoning, and what we believe. Critical studies of human culture and of ideologies reveal how great an influence propaganda, the media, and advertising exert on peoples' beliefs and outlooks. We now have a huge body of documentation, particularly from the Nazi period, on the devilish ways that reasoning deteriorates into rationalization for the most despicable of purposes.[7] Further, through depth psychology, we have become aware of the role of the unconscious in determining these rationalizations.

7: Lucy S. Dawidowicz, *The War against the Jews, 1933–1945* (New York: Bantam, 1975).

The same modernity in which the principle of autonomy was so crucial later gave rise to self-correcting stances. These critical stances now challenge the notion of a rational free-standing autonomy in ways that the early sages of the Reform rabbinate could not have foreseen. The notion of a sure bond between reason and autonomy has been discredited. The idea of a free, untrammeled, above-it-all, disinterested, transcendent reason has been revealed as an illusion, not only to be distrusted, but methodically so. The philosopher Paul Ricoeur aptly coined the phrase "the hermeneutics of suspicion" to describe all those forms of interpretation and analysis now familiar to us—Freudian, Marxist, structuralist, and, most recently, feminist—that have analyzed and reduced both conscious and unconscious processes of "reason" into motivations that in a large part have little to do with rational or "noble" principles or morality itself.

For Jews, this problem is even more acute because of the history of our times. The identification of modernity with the reason of ancient Athens was not sufficient to ward off the Holocaust. Heidegger, the leading philosopher of Germany, a nation that prided itself on rational philosophies, joined the Nazis early on. Many learned university professors in all fields did the same. Science and technology, offsprings of reason, which have produced marvels in the realm of healing, communications, and transportation, were also harnessed without any regard to degree of cruelty or beastliness to the murder of vast numbers of human beings with the least residue possible.

At the very beginning of our modern age, among the most rational characters depicted in Shakespeare's plays, those who speak for autonomous reason against all authority, are also among the worst villains. Edmund in *King Lear* and the archvillain Iago in *Othello*, the supreme rationalist who appeals continuously to reason, are at the same time *homini emancipati a Deo*, people whose autonomous selves are constituted of a bundle of self-seeking purposes, free from any system of moral value, obligation, or authority.

Idolatry

A consideration of the relationship between idolatry and autonomy leads us directly to a more balanced view of autonomy in the hierarchy of liberal Judaic values. Modern historic consciousness has helped us to recognize that potential in the elevation of autonomy—personal choice—to the height of an overarching religious principle is the danger of idolatry. All idolatry is ultimately reducible to the worship of self, or an aspect of one's self separated from anything beyond. This is, of course, apparent in the idolatries of our own time: the worship of money, material possessions, power, position, honor and fame, or its lesser cousin, celebrity, to which so many people in our society devote their lives and their means. The encouragement of the worship of any state or political party as the highest arbiter of personal behavior is also an aspect or projection of self-interest. Autonomy, too, when raised to the level of religious principle detached from limitations imposed by consideration of other religious values and mindless of any authority beyond itself, is no exception. This applies especially in a time in which there is widespread contempt for the very idea of any authority beyond the atomistic self.

Just as with the deification of reason as God among politically triumphant exponents of the French Enlightenment,[8] so the exaltation of autonomy as the central self-defining, primal principle of Reform Judaism—its distinguishing mark—in comparison with other constructs of Judaism, has created a god bound to fail, with the inevitable demoralizing consequences of all failed idolatries. In the early history of Reform Judaism in Europe, as well as in the twentieth century in America, Reform Judaism adopted the categories of the "rational," "civilized," "enlightened" as criteria not only for Jewish social or public behavior in dress and manner but also for the content and form of Jewish religious expression. This is in no small part due to the fact that the public debate among the non-Jewish elite over whether the Jews should be emancipated, tolerated, legally accorded political, social, and economic rights was often conducted around the question: Are Jews sufficiently "enlightened" or "civilized" to enter civil society? In response, spokesmen of early Reform Judaism used the very words "civilized," "rational," "enlightened" to describe Jewish values. Changes were made in Jewish forms of worship, in the physical structure of the synagogue, and in prayer texts not only for the purpose of aesthetic refinement of worship or out of greater commitment to prophetic moral

---

8: An actual Festival of Reason took place at Notre Dame Cathedral in Paris on November 10, 1793, the culmination of a formidable de-Christianization movement (cf. Leo Gershay, *The French Revolution and Napoleon* [New York: Appleton Century Crofts, 1933], 287).

ideas that early Reformers considered to be the core of Judaism. In many cases changes were made to conform to the aesthetics and forms of Western European civility because of the drive for Jewish social and economic acceptance and advancement.[9] A number of particular Jewish religious practices then considered to be embarrassing because they were "different" were radically changed or eliminated in subordination to the prevailing culture. Sacred texts that had been cherished by generations of Jews were deemed "backward," "superstitious," and "benighted" and therefore to be cast aside.[10]

The Anglo-Saxon West had developed an ideology of its superiority over the "native East" to justify colonial conquest and economic exploitation of African and Asiatic lands and people. Modernizing Jews, unconsciously absorbing this ideology, took the same attitude and adopted the very words Western scholars used to describe the "savage" cultures of native peoples to dismiss many Jewish religious practices and texts that Jewish reformers considered noxious accretions to the original pure moral and enlightened rational core of Judaism. Studies produced by Jews under the aegis of the Enlightenment and even taught in liberal rabbinic schools well into the twentieth century took the same views of hallowed Jewish practices, such as the use of the shofar, breaking the glass at a wedding, *Havdalah*, as that of Western scholars analyzing the relics of ancient barbarous superstitions. Reform rabbis themselves often made use of the very term of the Western ideology of conquest and exploitation—namely, "orientalism"—to reject aspects of "backward (Eastern as opposed to Western) religious practices." Some reform rabbis claimed to have "led their congregations out of orientalism." In fact, the endeavor by German or Western Jews to make clear-cut distinctions between themselves and their Eastern European counterparts describing the latter as *Ostjuden* (Eastern European Jews) was tainted with the same mentality. Since Judaism itself and Jews are in fact from "the East," this was a form of unconscious Jewish self-hate absorbed from non-Jewish, anti-Semitic, Anglo-Saxon Western culture.

All of this is understandable in the context of the cultural crisis brought about by the possibilities and challenges of the Emancipation. A non-Jewish scholar, John Murray Cuddihy, has called this challenge

---

9: Stefan C.Reif, *Judaism and Hebrew Prayer* (Cambridge University Press, 1993), 270.
10: Among these, kabbalistic and halachic texts and commentaries.

"the ordeal of civility" and argues that Jews in modernity have been able to be innovators by virtue of being outside the "establishment."[11] But sacrifice of identity out of the desire for acceptance and inclusion falls within the shadow of idolatry. We must be wary, in our time, of similar motives.

It is all the more compelling, then, to recall that throughout Scripture, personal choice in religious matters—what we would call the exercise of autonomy on the basis of principle and integrity—is, for the most part, linked with the struggle *against* idolatry:

> Behold I set before you this day a blessing and a curse: the blessing, if you hearken to the commandments of the Lord your God, which I command you this day, and the curse, if you will not hearken to the Lord your God but turn aside out of the way which I command you this day, to go after other gods.
>
> (Deuteronomy 11:26–28)

Consistently in Scripture (see Isaiah 44:17–20) and subsequently among the ancient rabbis as well, it is idolatry that leads us away from the ability to make the proper moral or religious choices! Many modern thinkers, Jewish and non-Jewish as well, have now long emphasized the sense of "the Other." The more we transcend our own self-interest, the more we are free to choose or, using our term, the more autonomous we become.[12]

Seemingly a paradox, autonomy as choice against idols is choosing the path of being true to ourselves. According to the prophetic reading, and throughout the history books of the Bible, the ancient Israelites were subjected to the seductions of the materially advanced and sophisticated culture they encountered in Canaan. They often succumbed to it, with the result of moral and spiritual corruption. The best of what the Jewish people, always a minority, have achieved and contributed to the world has often resulted from a struggle against the pressure of the majority, the temptation of "making it" in whatever the dominant culture. Further, according to Jewish tradition, a higher and

---

11: John Murray Cuddihy, *The Ordeal of Civility* (New York: Basic Books, 1974).

12: Chanoch of Alexsandrow (1798–1870), an early hasidic rabbi, on heteronomy: "Others gain control over you only to the extent that you have hasidic will other than God's."

greater degree of autonomy is achieved through the practice of the mitzvot.

Autonomy requires practice. That is an insight of the Jewish tradition. The prophets and sages of Israel called that discipline the practice of mitzvot. According to the faith of modernity, reason itself would inevitably bring about the spiritual and moral refinement of human beings and make us more free to choose. According to Rabban Gamliel, the spiritual refinement of humanity derives from the practice of mitzvot. In the drama *A Man for All Seasons*, a young man about to be suborned into an act particularly disloyal and treacherous against an innocent man who had befriended and helped him tells the authority who is bribing him that it is a very hard thing for him to do. The official answers: "The next time it will be easier." The opposite holds true as well. Mitzvah leads to mitzvah.

The Judaic archetypal image of the autonomous individual is, of course, Abraham. "When he was one, I called him" (Isaiah 51:2). The ancient rabbinic realization of the model of the autonomous individual is contained in two celebrated stories imbedded in the Jewish consciousness. The first is, of course, about the young Abraham as iconoclast, idol breaker in his father's idol shop,[13] applicable to us in the light of the theologian Paul Tillich's comment that our society is a perfect factory of idols. On the positive side, complementing this *via negativa* toward God's way, is the story told of the young Abraham who persisted in seeking the highest in existence that he could serve and always rejecting the lesser.[14] This is autonomy as the struggle against idols.

Balancing Autonomy

Short of abandoning the principle of autonomy, what countervailing measures can we apply to avoid a self-indulgent form of idolatry? It is the commendable anxiety of this question that I believe is behind the discussions among liberal Jews around the question of "limits," "boundaries," and the sources of authority in liberal Judaism itself. It is sincere grappling with this issue that led Eugene Borowitz to speak of a

---

13: Friedman, ed., *Tanna de-Bei Eliyyahu*, 27–28; *Genesis Rabbah* 38:13.
14: A. Jellinek, ed., *Bet ha-Midrash* 2:118ff.

Jewish covenantal, communal self, implying obligation to the Jewish people, faithfulness to its past and concern for its future. Nevertheless, if we are not to fall into the idolatry of the "voice of the people as the voice of God," we cannot accept literally or easily in our current situation that the Jewish people "will know what to do."

As a youth I was taught, and as a young man I taught others, that it is even more difficult to be a Reform Jew than a traditional Jew because in order to exercise autonomy, personal choice, we have to know a good deal more than the "blindly accepting" Orthodox. And yet, even as the principle of autonomy has been accorded among us greater and greater validity, accepted as an undiscussed "given" of Reform Judaism, even repeated like a mindless mantra, who of us will claim that we, or our children, are taught more or know more about Judaism than a comparable Orthodox or Conservative Jew? How can we be certain that our choices are made more on the basis of knowledge and principle or of living in behalf of the sovereignty of God than out of convenience, or lack of knowledge, or other reasons that are self-serving and therefore idolatrous?

It is, in our time, insufficient to rely on communal choice in order to find the way of God. We cannot say of our present-day Jewish community that they will find the right way, as Hillel was able to say of the actively practicing Jews of his time: "If they are not prophets then they are descendants of prophets." It has taken thousands of years of immersion in Torah and in living a Jewish way of life to create in the individual Jewish consciousness those innate reflexive responses such as sensitivity to the poor and the powerless and basic human decency in relationships with others. Considering the cataclysmic breaks that have taken place in the continuities of our religious heritage in the twentieth century, and the low level of Jewish knowledge and observance among Reform Jews at present, reliance on communal decision making is a weak reed on which to lean in walking the path of God.

One can understand in our circumstances this emphasis on community as our source of authority. For reasons outside the scope of this essay, there has emerged in our time an American Jewish ethnicity, a civil religion, which has emphasized loyalty to peoplehood, the centrality of the State of Israel, the authority of the central communal fundraising structures. We do so even though for the most part we have an oligarchy, not a democracy, of Jewish communal leadership. For a time this civil religion has supported Jewish communal coherence. But in the absence of a religious, a Torah, core to Jewish identity, this current Jewish identity structure has now become in many ways detrimental to Jewish continuity in the United States. Furthermore, this civil religion is often in conflict with core Judaic religious principles of great value to liberal Judaism. This is evident in the call for unquestioned support for the policies of any government of Israel at any given time, no matter what those policies are or the breach of moral principles that a given policy represents, or how destructive it is even to other aspects of Jewish spirituality. With regard to the policies of the State of Israel, only on the issue of religious pluralism has Reform Jewry risen to challenge the unquestioning stance of Jewish united fund-raising, the major interest of which is, of course, not to threaten the fund-raising structure itself.

While Borowitz has seen the need for an autonomy based in covenant obligation, his emphasis has been on peoplehood. But in our time, communal consciousness alone is as insufficient as the autonomy of the individual self. Autonomy as the struggle against idols can be found only in a covenantal community that is immersed in Torah, our religious heritage known and lived. If we say, as does Borowitz, that our autonomy emerges from a covenantal relationship with God, then we must remember that Torah, the vast accumulation of sacred texts through the ages that have achieved authoritative status with Jewish communities over many centuries, is the core mediation of divine revelation to Jews. It is in Torah that Jews over the ages have found the divine encounter and divine guidance. Among some Reform rabbis and academicians this direction has been expressed in the idea of an "exegetical community." This means a community that regularly, as a way of life, studies Torah and practices mitzvot in a conscious and conscientious manner. This implies the emergence of a growing number of Jews in all walks of life immersed in Torah, our heritage, which would truly bring into being a covenantal community.

There is another great value in the American Jewish "turn to Torah" beginning to take place now as central to Jewish life. And that is because Torah texts provide us with a "culture-critical" state of mind. The anthropologist of structural analysis, Claude Lévi-Strauss, once noted after teaching in the United States for some time that students here were always intent on the prestige of the "latest" theory, the "newest" methodology, and disregarded all else. In the same way, for a long time Reform Jews have prided themselves on keeping up with the most current trends. Catering to current cultural values and then looking for sources in our texts that seem to accord with them, much Jewish scholarship and many rabbinic sermons have been devoted to showing the compatibility of this or that element in the Jewish heritage with whatever was the current "leading edge." In this way, Torah became more Kantian than Kant, more Freudian than Freud, and recently, more preoccupied with dysfunctional family life than the talk shows. This tendency has made current culture the standard by which Judaism measures itself.Should we dare to say that our teachers should reverse this process and make Torah the measure and standard to which current culture should adhere?

One of the great benefits of Torah as a way of informing autonomous choices and keeping us from idolatry is that Torah has emerged over many centuries in so many different cultures and climes that it can become a way par excellence of testing the current culture. Thus Torah provides a safeguard to autonomy as a choice against idols, helping us to think less reactively and subserviently to current culture and to become far more critical of it. For example, the emphasis on prophetic literature that once infused the Reform rabbinic curriculum for many years did develop among Reform Jews, both rabbis and laypeople, a stance of sensitivity to injustice, corruption, and hypocrisy in the contemporary culture.

Concluding Thoughts

First, it is important that the discussion of autonomy increasingly move out of the academic realm and into the forums of our people. The origins of the concept of autonomy, its actual meanings, the problems associated with the concept as a divining mark of any form of Judaism deserve much wider discussion.

Second, should not our leadership, at least as a countervailing balance to the overwhelming emphasis on self-interest in our culture, bring more of an emphasis in religious teaching to mitzvot as obligation that focuses on purposes beyond the self and its narrow satisfactions? Recently, a study was made about Jewish worship among lay people under an official auspice of the Central Conference of American Rabbis. The questions asked, the tone of the study overall, could be summed up in the question "What do you get out of worship?" As an entirely appropriate way of setting the tone or direction of the questionnaire, it could also have included these questions: "Do you feel more committed as a Jew as a result of worship? Does the worship service motivate you to the service of God and your fellow human beings? Does it strengthen your moral fiber?"

As to the form and content of Jewish religious observance, at least as a balance to the tremendous emphasis on discovering more and more grounds for the legitimation of the autonomous self as a leading principle of Reform Judaism, perhaps we should take up again the project of fashioning Reform principles of a liberal *halachah,* which could help us create real religious community, not an unimportant need of Jews today. It may be valuable to return also to our project of fashioning liberal Jewish guidelines for the creative retrieval of our text and observances. For example, ancient dietary laws of *kashrut* brought the elemental human need for nurture into the religious realm. Are we able to read and interpret practices of *kashrut* in our own way? These might be related to cruel practices or economic exploitation in the preparation of foods as well as the symbolic meaning of certain foods to the Jewish community. Rabbi Richard Levy, a president of the Central Conference of American Rabbis, has made suggestions along these lines. But we have not as yet crafted a liberal Jewish hermeneutic or method of interpretation of Torah that could serve powerfully to spiritualize all aspects of life, those particularly that modernity may have excluded from the realm of religion.

All of this hinges on defining the center of Jewish life not in a geographic location, nor in some office, nor in some communal organization, nor certainly in the impulses of individuals, but in what has been the center of the people of Israel through the ages, the bond of our people, our reason for being and the means and purpose of our continuity, namely, Torah, our religious heritage known and lived.

❧ SEVEN ❧

Mending the World
and the Evil Inclination:
The Human Role in Redemption

MICHAEL S. STROH

Redemption (*geulah*) and messianism (*meshichiyut*) have been primary categories of Jewish faith since talmudic times. Messianism, the belief in the coming of the messiah or the Messianic Age, breaks the cycle of endless repetition characteristic of the ancient pagan world. Just as the seasons repeat themselves endlessly, so life is a cycle of repetitions and nothing new ever appears. War and injustice will never come to an end. Our broken world, desperately in need of repair, cannot be fixed. Death is the inescapable fact of existence. Messianism breaks this unending cycle and is committed to the belief that life has a direction and a purpose. A day will come when "nation will not lift up sword against nation, neither will they continue to learn the arts of war" (Isaiah 2:4). Our broken world does have a *tikkun,* a repair.

Messianism also speaks to the redemption of suffering and the meaning of death. The Jewish tradition is committed to the idea that God will give life to the dead (*mechayeh ha-metim*). Even if this is not taken literally, it tells us that in the struggle of the forces of life against the forces of death, life ultimately conquers death, no matter what we see with our eyes. Suffering and death are not an add-on to human life, they are part of the essential structure of life itself. Like life, they are mysterious. The idea of *olam haba*, the next world, is also a component of messianism. The concept of messianism has had a major impact on the entire conceptual structure of Western civilization.

The system of mitzvot (commandments) is not an end in itself but leads to redemption; thus, they have ultimate meaning and purpose. Another phrase is *tikkun olam*, which means "the mending of the world." The phrase *l'takken olam b'malchut Shaddai*, to mend the world under the sovereignty of God, also has messianic implications. Since Judaism is a religion of commandments, we ask: What is the human capacity to fulfill the commandments? In other words, to what extent are human beings capable of bringing redemption, "the days of the Messiah," of leading the world to the sovereignty of God?

In the Jewish tradition there are mitzvot concerning relations between a person and one's neighbor (*bein adam l'rei'eihu*) and between a person and God (*bein adam l'Makom*). This is roughly the distinction between ethical and ritual commandments. Judaism has raised the question of our participation in redemption in regard to both ethical and ritual mitzvot. In this essay, I am mostly concerned with human ethical capacity, but I think it is also important to ask in what way the Jewish fulfillment of ritual commandments contributes to the redemption of the world.

The Enlightenment bequeathed to us a belief in the infinite perfectibility of humanity and the corollaries that human beings are self-sufficient and that progress is steady and inevitable. The idea of progress was understood as an ever-expanding human horizon, not only technologically, but morally, and that what we call "the days of the Messiah," redemption, would be achieved by humanity alone. God was unnecessary for this process. Reform Judaism, being a post-Enlightenment expression of Jewish faith and much influenced by its ideas, shared this belief in the ability of unaided humanity to create a perfectly just world. This is certainly reflected in the Pittsburgh Platform of 1885 when it says: "We recognize in the modern era of universal heart and intellect the approaching of the realization of Israel's great messianic hope for the establishment of the kingdom of truth, justice, and peace among all men." The Reform belief in the idea of a Jewish mission to lead the world to social justice and the strong Reform commitment to social action also flow from this idea.

The Enlightenment belief in human capacity began to crumble after World War I for Europeans, but it took World War II for the impact to be felt in America. Christian theology after World War I reflected the disillusionment with the Enlightenment faith in the essential goodness of humanity and its progress to a perfect world of peace and justice. For Jews, the Holocaust was the last blow to Enlightenment philosophy; it became impossible for Jews to understand how the home of learning and culture, the birthplace of Kant and Hegel, could produce Nazism and bring it to power. After Auschwitz, what Jew could be comfortable with an easy optimism about human goodness and the human capacity for moral progress?

Judaism believes in a *b'rit*, a partnership between God and the Jewish people and a *b'rit* between God and humanity. What are the terms of this partnership? What is the human role? What is God's role? Has there been any moral progress since the dawn of humanity? How much can human beings do to bring the Messiah? Does everything depend on God? What is the particular Jewish role in bringing redemption? If we have become disillusioned with human perfectibility, what happens to the Reform commitment to social action?

These are among the most significant questions that liberal religious Jews are asking themselves as history moves from the Enlightenment era to a new phase of the human drama that some have called "postmodern." As the first phase of Reform Judaism is ending, and we become the architects of the transition to the second phase, we ask ourselves: Can we create a post-Enlightenment, yet liberal, Jewish theology? There are those who say that post-Enlightenment disillusionment requires a return to fundamentalism, and this call is being heard in many religions, including Judaism. For some, disillusionment with the values of the Western world and its moral chaos lead to the belief that only a full rupture with the heritage of the Enlightenment can save humanity. Fundamentalist Christians, Muslims, and Jews respond favorably to this message and their impact is increasing. It may be that the confrontation to come will be between Western values and religious fundamentalism. Total rejection of Western values is not a message that liberals can affirm; there are real gains from the Enlightenment, such as democracy, that we want to hold on to. While we can no longer accept Enlightenment philosophy whole cloth, we do not want to abandon it totally either. We want to preserve some aspects of the Enlightenment and reject others. Some believe this is impossible, but the viability of liberal religion in the future will depend on it. We are committed to the position that fundamentalism is not the answer. Where do we go from here?

The Siddur understands the notion of God as redeemer to be a basic Jewish belief. *Mi chamochah ba-elim Adonai*, "Who is like You, Eternal One among the gods," says the third blessing of the *Shema* section of the service. This blessing ends with the words, *Baruch Atah Adonai ga'al Yisrael*, "Praised are You, Adonai, who has redeemed Israel." The redemption referred to is the saving of Israel from the approaching Egyptians when they crossed the Sea of Reeds. Thus, the miracle at the Sea became a fixed part of the expression of Jewish monotheism, and God's action in history to redeem the Jewish people at the Exodus became the model for God's continuing redemptive activity. This refers not only to the redemption from Egypt but to God's continual redemption in every generation.

At no point in the Torah can the Pharaoh let the Jews go, for then he would be responsible for our redemption. Neither is Moses the redeemer or we would worship Moses and not God. The Torah tells us that we were redeemed through God's actions alone. The Passover haggadah tells the same tale. The Exodus is the model for an ongoing redemption: "In every generation a tyrant has arisen who threatened to destroy us." Had God not saved us, we would not be here now. The haggadah is a story of redemption; it is about the meaning and purpose of human history. It is a path that takes us "from bondage to freedom, from agony to joy, from mourning to festivity, from darkness to light, from servitude to redemption."[1] The haggadah is about redemption through liberation, redemption through God's action. For the haggadah, this is the purpose of human history.

This does not mean that Jews are passive in the process of redemption. That God gave commandments presumes we have the capacity to fulfill them. Our sin is not our incapacity but that we can fulfill them and choose not to. The extent of human participation in the redemptive process is debated in Jewish literature and the answers vary from a sudden cataclysmic divine act, when things have become so bad they cannot get any worse, to the Lurianic Kabbalah in which Jews performing mitzvot liberate divine sparks and help move history to the Messianic Age. Irving Greenberg points out that Jews progressively become more active partners in the *b'rit*. In the Torah, God issues absolute commands and Jews must obey them. But the Talmud is a series of debates about what the commandments are; there is human input and much disagreement. Ultimately, it is human beings who determine the content of the commandments.

It is an important insight of our tradition that God's action still leaves room for human activity. It is striking how much the Jewish tradition

---

1: Herbert Bronstein, ed. , *A Passover Haggadah: The New Union Haggadah* (New York: Central Conference of American Rabbis, 1974), 57.

empowers human beings, and this message is repeated again and again in Talmud and *midrash*. This is best expressed in the famous story in the Talmud about a debate about the purity of the oven of Achnai. In the end even a voice from heaven (*bat kol*) does not persuade the rabbis. They make their own decision contrary to the heavenly voice on the grounds of *lo bashamayim hi*, the Torah is not in heaven.[2] In other words the Torah now belongs to human beings and it is human beings who must determine its meaning. Utter passivity is not required of Jews, either in textual interpretation or in action in the world, in order to be religious.

The struggle over human activity is being fought again in the religious controversy over Zionism. While some believe that Zionism is a sin because it expresses lack of trust in God and the coming of the Messiah, others believe that Jewish action is part of the messianic process. This controversy still rages in Israel and the Jewish world. For liberal Jews, there is no question that Judaism does not require total Jewish passivity.

Post-Enlightenment thinkers, however, introduced a new dimension to this discussion, namely, that of God's passivity. They exchanged human passivity for divine passivity. The idea that God plays no active role in redemption resulted in liturgical change. In the *Union Prayer Book*[3] and continued in *Gates of Prayer*,[4] the word *goel* (redeemer) was changed to *geulah* (redemption). A continuous historical process was substituted for God's action. The notion of God, who acts to save us in every generation, was replaced by the idea of human progress. Similarly, *mashiach* (Messiah) was replaced by *y'mot ha-mashiach* (days of the Messiah). While it is true that we have many problems with the idea of a personal Messiah who is a male king and that "days of the Messiah" is a traditional phrase, the result was to conceive of the Messianic Age as a goal to be reached through human progress alone. In the *Aleinu* prayer in the Siddur, we find the words *al ken n'kaveh l'cha Adonai Eloheinu*, "We, therefore, place our hope in You, Adonai our God." In You, not in ourselves! In the *Gates of Prayer* translation of this verse, however, we are asked "to share the pain of others, to heed Your call for

2: Irving Greenberg, "The Third Great Cycle of Jewish History," *Perspectives: A CLAL Thesis* (New York: The National Center for Learning and Leadership, 1980), 6.

3: *The Union Prayer Book* (New York: Central Conference of American Rabbis, 1959), 19.

4: *Gates of Prayer: The New Union Prayer Book* (New York: Central Conference of American Rabbis, 1975), 60.

justice, to pursue the blessing of peace. . . ."[5] In other words, we, guided by God's vision, will lead the world to justice and peace. We still say "*Oseh shalom bimromav . . .*" "May God who creates peace in the heavens create peace for us. . . ." But do we believe universal peace to be a purely human endeavor, or does God play a role in this for us?

Hegel and Darwin bequeathed to us the belief in evolutionary progress. Everything evolves from lower to higher, all things get better and better. In this process God is unnecessary, either history will move to its inevitable redemptive conclusion through human good will, finally liberated from the barbarism of all history prior to the Enlightenment, or history itself will reach this end through its own internal laws. The last philosophy to espouse a belief in the iron laws of history leading to an inevitable goal of happiness and plenty was Marxism.

In his book *Judaism and Modern Man* (1951), Will Herberg, former Marxist and then committed religious Jew, comments:

> In 1871, Algernon Charles Swinburne, the poet of the "new freedom," hailed man in words that brought a thrill of pride to the "emancipated" minds of the day: "Glory to Man in the highest,/The maker and master of things" (Hymn to Man). Today, not much more than three-quarters of a century later, poets and publicists are proclaiming the "end of the human race." In his brief reign as "master of things," man has brought himself and his universe to the brink of destruction. . . . Never in all recorded history has the collapse of the hopes of a civilization taken place so suddenly, almost in the sight of one generation. . . . In its chaos, insecurity, and all-pervading sense of disaster, the world of today is more akin to the world of 912, to the Dark Ages a thousand years ago, than to the world of 1912, which some of us can still remember. [6]

Algernon Charles Swinburne could not anticipate either Auschwitz or Hiroshima. It is a common misconception that Judaism believes that people are basically good. Traditional Jewish belief about human nature is that the human heart is a scene of struggle between the good and evil inclination; the evil inclination is stronger, and the good incli-

---

5: Ibid., 620.

6: Will Herberg, *Judaism and Modern Man* (New York: Harper Torchbooks, 1951), 3.

nation needs assistance from outside. The evil inclination has proved more intractable than the believers in an early dawn of the Messianic Age could foresee. We have been witness in our time to the collapse of all the "end of days" ideologies that predicted redemption through human beings alone: socialism, communism, and even the kibbutz ideal. Where do we stand in the God–human partnership? There are three alternatives:

1. God is unnecessary. The world will slowly (or quickly) move toward redemption. This will be accomplished by humanity alone.
2. Humanity can do little or nothing. God will bring redemption when God wills.
3. Humanity can, although imperfect and sinful, participate in redemption through obedience to God's commands. Nonetheless, humanity cannot do everything. God must fulfill the task.

Traditionally, Judaism comes closest to the third choice. The first belief in human perfectibility, while believed by many in the recent past, has fallen on hard times. The second possibility finds little Jewish resonance; even the most skeptical about human capacity still believes in the ability to obey mitzvot, to do good. The real question, then, is how much can we expect of humanity? The answer to that question may not be known until the end of human history. What we do know is that we are commanded to keep striving, and we must believe we are capable of following the commandments, with God's help.

It is, I believe, becoming clear that social action must be religiously based. If social action and ethical activism are not religiously grounded, then they are without any ground or basis and, perhaps, temporary. The path to a mended world may be longer than the post-Enlightenment thinkers anticipated, and sometimes hard to decipher. If our resolve is not to weaken, it must be based on religious faith. We strive, not because we see rapid results, but because ethical action is commanded by God. It is also God who promises fulfillment and redemption. Modern social philosophers such as Martin Buber and Ernst Bloch testify to the religious ground of human hope for ethical realization. Judaism has blessed us with a vision of a world redeemed, a world of peace, justice, and truth. It has gone further and affirmed God's conquest of death itself and the gathering of all humanity into the ultimate fulfillment in its language about the return of life to the dead (*t'chiat ha-metim*). While God acts, Judaism has not called us to merely sit and wait. Judaism is fully committed to the meaning of life in this world and it places mitzvot at the center of its religious activity. Judaism has this dialectic, believing both in human responsibility to fulfill the mitzvot and God's action as redeemer.

We have asked about the role of humanity as God's partner in redemption. We have pursued questions about the human capacity for evil and the basis of hope for a mended world. We have tried to discover a faith profound enough to believe in human striving and offer a realistic hope for the future. We want to believe that messianism is not an illusion. We want to be able to do this in the face of Auschwitz. We have asked these universal questions, but we have not yet asked about a particular Jewish role in this process. Judaism is a tension between universalism and particularism, a dimension that comprehends all humanity and a dimension of Jewish inwardness. We exist as a real people in history with a language and a land. In the words of Leo Baeck, what is the purpose of the existence of "this people Israel"?

The Jewish tradition teaches us that *mashiach* arises from Israel. Whether we say Messiah or Messianic Age, *mashiach* or *y'mot ha-mashiach*, do we believe that a time of justice and peace for all humanity arises uniquely from the Jewish people? What specific role does the Jewish people play in the messianic process? Franz Rosenzweig believed that the Jewish people has a unique responsibility to keep the lamp burning, to live in its particularism. History does not belong to Judaism, he said, it belongs to Christianity. The end of history, however, belongs to Judaism. Christianity and, therefore, the world are moving to the place where Judaism already is. Even now, if the Jews were to disappear, Christianity would descend into paganism. Judaism and the Jewish people are essential for redemption. It is our unique responsibility to continue to be what we are.

Perhaps the Jewish people has a special mandate through our prophetic heritage to work for social justice. Can we really say that Jews have a greater obligation than the rest of humanity to be moral? Is this not a human obligation? How can our particularity consist in doing what every human being should do? It is difficult to believe that Judaism teaches that Jews have a stronger obligation than all others to be ethical; surely we call upon all humanity to strive for justice.

Perhaps what is unique is not our obligation to be ethical, but our teaching that the center of religion is ethics; it is our particular message for the world that justifies our particular existence. If we examine the historical record, is it not true that only religions that grow out of Torah—Judaism, Christianity, and Islam—have a concept of this-worldly redemption? Does any culture or philosophy not based on Torah, for example, that of ancient Greece, have any concept of repentance—a necessary component of ethical activism—or historical change, or messianism? Perhaps, indeed, the message of Torah is unique.

One of the most significant issues of modern Jewish thought is the justification for the continued separate, particular existence of Israel as a religious people. Clearly Judaism's commitment to the ultimate meaning of life in this world, that human striving is not in vain and will reach fulfillment, is a fundamental teaching of Jewish faith. Life is not "a tale/ Told by an idiot, full of sound and fury,/ Signifying nothing" (*Macbeth*), nor is this world a meaningless place in which we are tested until our spirits go elsewhere? No other religion is so committed to the redemption of this world in both its spiritual and physical dimensions as is Judaism. Mitzvot as the center of Jewish religion make Judaism into a religion of this-worldly redemption. We cannot flee from this world because we are commanded to transform it. In the face of Auschwitz and Hiroshima, Bosnia and Somalia, we believe this because our belief comes from God and not from this world itself. We can act, but without God there is no redemption. The exact proportions of the God–human mix, however, are mysterious.

Franz Rosenzweig was right, too. Even though most of the world accepts the message of Isaiah that "nation shall not lift up sword against nation, neither shall they continue to learn the arts of war," still the purpose of the Jewish people on earth has not been fulfilled. Our particularity, our awesome history, our very existence are mysterious and we do fulfill a purpose by keeping the lamp burning.

We end in the proper place: mystery. There is much we do not understand. What we do understand is that God is a God who commands; God is a God who, as the Exodus story tells us, liberates slaves. God has called us *l'takken olam b'malchut Shaddai*, "to mend the world under the sovereignty of the Almighty." A belief in a self-sufficient humanity, moving inexorably to a perfect world has proven to be not only shallow but, in the face of Auschwitz, offensive. To believe this, in my opinion, in the face of recent and current history would require a greater leap of faith than any traditional religious teaching. What will prevent us from retreating into quietism and waiting for God to make everything right, total passivity in the face of great evil, is the Jewish belief in our partnership with God.

The belief that humanity can eradicate the evil inclination from the human heart by itself and that God is unnecessary is *hubris* or *chutzpah*. In contrast, Judaism teaches that God commands and we are called to fulfill these mitzvot. The movement of history from the present age to the age of the Messiah is, indeed, mysterious, but Judaism teaches us the realism of this hope. *P'tach libi b'toratecha u'v'mitzvotecha tirdof nafshi*, "Open my heart to Your Torah that my spirit may pursue Your commandments."

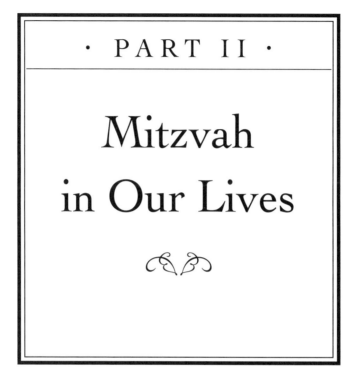

· PART II ·

Mitzvah in Our Lives

Brushes with the Sacred:
An Experiential Approach to Mitzvah

NILES E. GOLDSTEIN

The Problem

Let's be honest. American Jews in general (and liberal Jews in particular) have been lax for decades now in the observance of religious rituals. Many of us try to be good people. We volunteer, we pay our taxes, we support worthy causes. But the ethical is not always identical with the religious. Though Jews as a group have a fairly respectable profile for moral behavior in this society, we make a much poorer showing in the area of *religiosity*, of commitment to those rites and traditions that are beyond the ken of rational explanation and universal application.

There are, I think, three main reasons for this laxity: intellectual ambivalence, cultural dismissiveness, and prioritization of our values. As products of modernity, Jews today have been raised with a worldview that polarizes reason and faith. We've been taught that only those beliefs or behaviors that can be justified through rational argument are "true," that nonprovable doctrines (such as messianism) and nonrational actions (such as laying *tefillin*) are somehow primitive or superfluous. Having been brought up with this mindset, is it any wonder that Jews have serious questions about the importance of a great many of their ancient practices—or, for that matter, about the value of organized religion itself?

The second reason for our problem with observance stems from the conflict between universalism and particularism. Modernity elevated more than just rationality over faith; it also held the interests of society as a whole superior to the concerns and needs of its constituent groups.

95

For the first time, Jews were invited to participate as equals in the culture around them, and they rushed at the chance. The university (a "universal" institution) swiftly eclipsed the yeshiva (a particularistic one) in attracting Jewish students; the secular courts, as opposed to the rabbinical courts, became the seats where legal judgments were now rendered. Anything that tended to separate or distinguish Jews from their neighbors (such as dietary laws or head coverings) grew less and less relevant to Jewish lives.

The third reason for our trouble with mitzvot relates to our priorities and interests. It takes work to be a Jew in the modern world. How can we make habits out of practices that we find uncompelling? As acculturated (and, in many cases, assimilated) Jewish Americans, we've bought into the values of modernity. Most of us have strong secular educations, but few of us have equally strong Jewish ones. We know Dante better than Deuteronomy, the Bill of Rights more than the Ten Commandments. We sing the national anthem by heart at sporting events, but we can't read Hebrew or recite our daily prayers. None of this is a question of intelligence, of course. It's a matter of priorities. Of passions and commitments. And our commitments usually lie elsewhere.

Despite the attractions of modernity that make religious observance difficult, it was easier for our parents and grandparents than it's been for us. They still had the pull of memory, history, and community to motivate much of their Jewish behavior. They were closer to the Old World than we are (some having been born there); they heard stories about the way things used to be; they lived in Jewish neighborhoods where peer pressure and community norms were often more powerful motivators than conviction.

For better or worse, we live in a different world, a world in which these forces have disappeared or are no longer sufficient. Yet we're starting to see that "being" Jewish without behaving Jewishly is less and less possible. What liberal Jews need now is a way to stay Jewish, a new and compelling rationale for religious practice. Without it, our form of Judaism will be untenable, based on little more than sentimentality and nostalgia that encase a dead past. Ours is an age of multiple truths and multiple narratives. Each of us needs to find his or her own Jewish story. Where can we find these stories? Where will we discover our unique Jewish voices? The answers rest in the realm of personal experience.

A Portrait of the Ascetic as a Young Man

Like most other philosophy majors, I graduated from college without a career plan and with serious doubts about the true value of organized religion. Thanks to my mentor and thesis advisor, a brilliant Catholic philosopher who specialized in medieval religious thought, I held on to a belief at least in the existence of God; as to the worth of the rites and rituals of religious institutions, however, I was highly skeptical. How could wearing a prayer shawl or using a rosary help us with our daily lives? Why would God care?

With some savings and a part-time job as a youth counselor at a Jewish community center, I moved to Boston to begin work on the Great American Novel. I gave myself one year to finish the book and to figure out what I wanted to do with my life. The writing, if mediocre, was easy. It was the decision about a lifetime vocation that proved to be the hardest part of my self-imposed goal.

I wrote during the day. But at night I read. Jewish books mostly, books written not by objective and disinterested scholars and philosophers, but by spiritual partisans. After four years of studying the words of religion's critics, I wanted to understand what it was like from the inside, from the perspective of those whose primary focus wasn't some abstract and universal notion of "truth," but the way believing Jews ought to live their lives. And, for the first time, I read the entire Torah. Not as literature, but as sacred text.

I wasn't yet aware of just what forces were driving me, but I sensed that something was beginning to happen in my soul. I felt the need to create various regimens for myself, rituals designed to contain and control the often tempestuous (and sometimes self-indulgent) impulses of a twenty-two-year-old. I was fresh out of college, so I was still skeptical of the many Jewish practices that were available to me. Better to create and experience practices myself, I thought. What did the rabbis know about struggle anyway?

I shaved my head. I refused to watch television. I spent long periods in isolation. I was drawn to asceticism, to the ideas of privation and denial. One book to which I was particularly attracted was *Duties of the Heart*, a work solely concerned with the Jew's inner life, written by a medieval rabbi named Bachya ibn Pakuda. I decided to spice my food only on Shabbat. In that way, every day, three times a day, for six days out of the week, I would be fulfilling (in my mind) the commandment to "remember the Sabbath." Rather than adding to the joy of the day itself, the ascetic in me would *detract* from the joy of the rest of the week.

As the level of my observance grew, so did the intensity of my spiritual life. But it was a very dark kind of spirituality. Intuition told me that being Jewish in solitude was going to prove problematic, that it would lead me into some pretty forlorn terrain. I began to pray with other Jews: I went to the Harvard Hillel, joined a local *chavurah*, met with rabbis from the region. Before my novel was finished, it gradually became clear to me that something was calling my soul to join, and to help lead, the Jewish community. My vocation wouldn't emerge, as I'd predicted it would, as the product of a well-reasoned decision. It would instead be a matter of compulsion.

The Last Frontier

The summer before I began rabbinical school, I took a trip to Alaska, the Last Frontier. I'd just finished my novel (and, along with it, exorcised a few of my inner demons), and in a couple of months I'd be in Jerusalem, beginning the five years of training that would turn me into a rabbi. But the summer was mine. I decided to go to Alaska, a place that had always held a kind of mystical fascination for me. I loved the wilderness. And I wanted Alaska to be my dark forest, the frontier that would sever me from a world of struggle and prepare me for the world of study and prayer I was about to enter.

I spent a few weeks wandering alone through the Inside Passage, a panhandle of islands and inlets in southeast Alaska that is accessible only by boat or plane. At the end of the month I hooked up with a small group of kayakers in Gustavus, a tiny village at the mouth of the frigid waters of Glacier Bay National Park. A floatplane dropped us off deep within the preserve, and we spent a week in our kayaks, camping on various shores and islands, as we made our way back out. We slept due to our exhaustion, but it wasn't easy. It was the time of Alaska's summer solstice, and so, without regard to our collective protestations, the sun never fully set.

My afternoons were filled with the spray of humpbacks and the play of harbor seals, my evenings with the moaning of wind and the howling of wolves. The glaciers were everywhere. First, I would see the icebergs, floating like blue candy and sometimes as tall as houses. Then, after I carefully circumnavigated them, I'd hear the thunder, the distant roar of ice blocks as they cracked off the faces of glaciers and crashed into the water below. Finally, chilled by the breezes that swept over their tops, I reached the tidewater glaciers themselves, rivers of white ice unraveling into the sea.

I felt as if I were a worshiper in a crystal temple. The sights, sounds, and textures of Glacier Bay seemed to carry with them a kind of sanctity. Yet there was nothing "Jewish" about the experience. I was going to be a rabbi, and, like a graffiti artist is compelled to leave his or her mark on a monument, I felt compelled to leave a Jewish signature on this holy place. When we had down time, and before I went to sleep, I'd turn to some of my required summer reading: a primer on biblical Hebrew grammar. But that was just study. I needed to find some ritual, some Jewish ritual, that gave this experience a religious meaning. Something that proved, at least to myself, that I for one wouldn't take this moment for granted. For me, the bay wasn't merely a product of natural laws. It was an expression of divine grace.

In Boston, I'd sealed candles, matches, and a small prayer book into a ziplock bag and stuffed them into my backpack. I knew that close to eight Friday nights would transpire during my time in Alaska. I wanted to observe Shabbat, even though I had no idea where I'd be on those nights or how exactly I'd observe it. One Friday fell during my kayak trip in Glacier Bay. Here was my chance. I figured that since I couldn't really wait for sunset, midnight was late enough to light Shabbat candles. Everyone else in the camp was asleep (though I was the only Jew around anyway). The swarms of mosquitoes and gnats that plagued us on dry land had quieted. I removed my headnet and put on a yarmulke. I stuck two candles into the sand and lit them. Then I began the blessing: *Baruch Atah Adonai . . ..*

I was a Jew alone on Shabbat in Alaska. I didn't have a congregation with me, but somehow I didn't feel lonely. I had a mitzvah, and that mitzvah linked me not only to my people and history but to my God. The commandment to kindle light in order to usher in Shabbat is an ancient one. Yet the power I felt from those two small flames transcended time and even space. Because I was open both to its beauty and its spiritual force, that light, that mitzvah, became a kiss from earth to heaven, a whisper from heaven to earth. It was my offer of gratitude and God's promise of presence. And it was a brush with the sacred I will never forget.

I returned to Alaska four years later. I had one more year to go before ordination and had spent the previous summer working in Fairbanks as that Jewish community's student rabbi. During the course of the internship, I'd become good friends with Dave van den Berg, a Floridian who'd left the Lower 48—as Alaskans call the rest of the continental United States—after college and now spent much of his time working as a professional wilderness guide. I met Dave (who wasn't Jewish) through a common friend, a rugby teammate of mine from my days at the Hebrew University in Jerusalem. He spoke to me that summer about his interest in dog mushing and introduced me to some of his huskies. I knew then and there that I'd have to come back to join him on one of his trips.

The only time I was able to get away from classes was during our spring recess, which ran through Passover. I arrived in Fairbanks in time for the seder, which was being held in the congregation's newly built synagogue. While I helped lead the seder, Dave was busy gathering all the food and gear we needed for our trip. (I'd given him a list of what I could and couldn't eat during Passover.) When I left the synagogue I made a practice run with a few of the dogs near Dave's cabin. I'd never been on a dogsled before, and I wiped out more than once as my team whisked me through the woods. The eyes of my dogs looked like white moons as the beam from my headlamp would occasionally hit them. I couldn't believe the focus with which the dogs ran—as if nothing in the world existed but the trail—and I longed for such focus in my religious life.

We left Fairbanks the next morning. Our plan was to mush through the White Mountains, an area to the north, sleeping in our tent and in vacant cabins along the way. Loading and unloading the dogs (a dozen of them) and the gear was much more work than I'd ever imagined, but by the middle of the afternoon we were ready to push into the mountains. The first few miles were uphill and exhausting. Dave and I had to get off our sleds and run to the side of them just so the dogs could bear their weight. When the trail leveled out, though, we hopped back on and coasted through the crisp Alaskan spring. The White Mountains, severe, ragged hunks of rock, were stunning. We made camp that first night at a cabin on Caribou Bluff, melting snow and giving water to our teams before we unpacked our own items.

Picture the scene: two young men, a pair of mushing sleds, and twelve barking huskies on a windswept bluff in the middle of the Arctic interior. Now add matzah to the picture. I was determined to observe Passover as best I could, given the circumstances, no matter how bizarre it looked. (Who'd notice, anyway?) The sun had started to set, and we were hungry. Dave fumbled for our dinner, and I broke out the first box of matzah that we'd carefully placed in a separate meal bag. I removed a single piece and stared at it. Comfort food. Believe it or not, the familiarity of that matzah, juxtaposed with the beautiful but barren environment in which I found myself, overwhelmed any of the usual misgivings I had about its taste. I imagined the Exodus from Egypt, the master story of Passover: the exhaustion, the hunger, the barrenness of the desert. I saw myself in the story. I felt myself there, in ways I'd never before experienced while sitting around the seder table. I said the two blessings over the matzah and ate it. For an instant, I was no longer a Jew living in twentieth-century America. I was part of the people of Israel and their eternal covenant with God.

Waters of Life

The power of mitzvot can be tremendous. They can inspire and elevate us, and they can sometimes bring us face to face with the transcendent. Often, however, our own personalities and dispositions affect the attractiveness of particular religious rituals. One Jew may be moved by the experience of worship but not by the laws of *kashrut*; another might enjoy celebrating *Havdalah* but not fasting on Tisha B'Av. What is important is that we are exposed to the full range of mitzvot, that we never fall prey to ignorance about our spiritual traditions. For many of us, there are Jewish practices we're not even aware of, mitzvot that could touch our hearts and transform our lives. The key is to immerse ourselves in at least the knowledge of them before we begin to make judgments about the kind of Jewish life we want to lead.

During my first year of rabbinical school, I participated in a different kind of immersion. I lived in Kiryat Shmuel, a neighborhood in Jerusalem. Every Friday afternoon, I'd buy food for Shabbat in the local markets, go to rugby practice at the Givat Ram stadium of Hebrew University, and then clean up for services. There were many synagogues near my apartment, and almost each week I'd try out a new one. Several of the synagogues had a *mikveh* (a ritual bath) attached to them. I'd been in a *mikveh* only once, built into the cleft of a mountain in the Galilee, while I was a college student in Israel three years before. It was a very powerful experience, but it had never occurred to me that ritual immersion could become a regular part of my religious life, especially of my Shabbat preparation. Taking a shower after practice somehow seemed to pale in comparison.

There was a *mikveh* down the street from my apartment, in the basement of a synagogue named Yad Tamar, that I especially liked. Though I was invariably viewed by the other bathers with some degree of suspicion (since I did not look the part of a typical *mikveh* user), I always looked forward to my weekly immersion. Shabbat started to seem somehow different, somehow purer—or maybe I was the one who had changed. When I moved back to the United States to continue my studies, it became too difficult to go to *a mikveh* every week: There just weren't enough of them close to me. I began to go much less frequently but always at least once every year during the Hebrew month of Elul, in preparation for the Days of Awe. While today it is mainly Jewish women who practice the mitzvah of immersion into a *mikveh*, it became one of the most essential and powerful mitzvot in my life.

The waters of the *mikveh* are referred to as *mayim chayim*, or "living waters." They must come from a natural source, like a spring, stream, or rainwater, and they must completely envelop the Jew who enters them. Not even the hair on a person's head should float above the surface. It was just this feature—the idea of envelopment, of engulfment—that made going to the *mikveh* such a powerful and meaningful mitzvah to me. Just as we wrap prayer shawls around ourselves before we pray, so do the waters of a *mikveh* wrap themselves around us as we descend the pool's steps and enter into their liquid world.

The *mikveh* is ultimately about renewal and rebirth. Yet, in order for something to be reborn, it must first die. One hasidic master compares the *mikveh* to the womb:

> The inner mindset you should have for immersion in the *mikveh* . . . when you double yourself over . . . like a fetus within its mother, and you are born as a new creation—[is that you are] giving up your soul to God.

To be naked and enveloped by water mirrors the condition of a fetus in its womb. Upon exit from the womb, the fetus—now an infant—emerges into a new life situation. Its prior state, its previous mode of existence, is over and done with, dead forever. Yet from this death comes a new state, a new form. A new *life*. In the spiritual context, to enter into the waters of a *mikveh* is to reenter the "waters" of the divine womb. As an act of repentence and purification, a person must give back—if only for a moment—his or her very being before reunion with God is possible. It is this self-sacrifice that leads, paradoxically, to self-preservation. That life, through God's mediation, will triumph over death (even if that victory must take place in the world to come) is one of the recurring teachings of the Jewish tradition. And rarely have I felt God's hand as palpably as within the marble walls of a *mikveh*.

Vision in the Mountains

The road that began for me in Los Angeles unraveled ahead over sagebrush and sand. I'd been driving for only a short time, and I still had a country to cross—the Rockies, the Badlands, the Plains—before I would make a brief stop at my parents' home in Chicago. My second year of rabbinical school had just ended. I was moving out to New York City to continue my coursework, and I had orders to report to Fort Monmouth, New Jersey, in two weeks to begin basic training as an Army chaplain. There was a lot to think about. Yet all I could do was think of her.

My first love had just broken up with me, and I was lost. Not according to the map, but in my soul. Stories about love and loss are nothing new, of course, and I'd heard plenty of them in the past. What most of those stories failed to convey to me, however, was just how disorienting and debilitating such experiences could be to a young man. I needed to experience loss myself before I could truly understand its pain. With my girlfriend I thought my life had it all: purpose, completeness, direction. When she was taken away from me (which is how, in my despair, I perceived the situation), I felt as if I were left with nothing. A soul standing naked and alone. Lost in the wilderness.

Religious rituals grew strangely burdensome. Praying became more and more difficult. The thoughts and emotions that had informed my life up to that point had been wrested from me, and I didn't know how to respond. The loss of a first love was bad enough, but the vastly more troubling problem was the ambiguity and confusion that had taken its place. I was training to become a rabbi, a religious leader; in my grief and uncertainty, however, I was turning away from religion itself. I knew I had to do something. To punctuate the loss. To regain my bearings.

Toward the middle of the summer I went again into the White Mountains—though this set was in New Hampshire, not Alaska. I brought a rain tarp, my sleeping bag, and a journal. No food or books. Not even a watch. Nothing to link me to the outside world. The plan, based on the Native American vision quest, was to spend three days and nights seeking insight alone in the wilderness, without food, shelter, or human contact. I'd fasted on Yom Kippur and Tisha B'Av for years, so I had some idea of what hunger tasted like. I wasn't intimidated by the fasting. It was the uncertainty of what I'd discover within.

I searched my map for a region as removed as possible from the more visited spots off Route 93, and settled on a place called the Pemigewasset Wilderness, an area dead in the center of the forest. After parking my car at the trailhead, I hiked in about six miles to the edge of a cluster of high outcroppings called the Cliffs. I didn't want to hike in any deeper because I was alone and because I figured that three days without food would take their toll on my return.

There was no flat ground anywhere, so I placed my tarp over a small and stony clearing just off the trail. Dark, thick trees and mosquitoes that grew thicker by the minute were my only companions. Suddenly it started to rain. Hard. I'd been there less than half an hour and already I had a problem. With nothing but a green tarp to keep me dry, I rolled it like a tobacco leaf around my body and backpack. I waited. The rain pelted the plastic with a rhythm that was almost hypnotic. I started to doze, and as I did, I noticed that inches above my head was a fly, upside down, motionless, and safe beneath a leaf of its own.

Odd things occurred. I'd fallen into a state in which I couldn't tell if I were asleep or awake. I think I was both at the same time. I heard sounds. The patter of paws. Steps. I felt encircled by other beings. Watched by them. Dreams and reality became porous, intermingling at will. I didn't feel alone. Nor did I feel secure. And when the rain ended and I emerged from my cocoon, unsure of how long or even whether I'd been asleep, the sensation inside me was difficult to name. It wasn't exactly fear. More like heedfulness.

The hardest part of my vision quest, it turned out, wasn't the fasting; after the first twenty-four hours, I wasn't really hungry at all. It was the boredom. And the burden of being with no one but myself. The writer John Haines comments that, in the wilderness, we come to see our lives "in a time measured not by clocks and calendars, but by the turning of a great wheel." With an exploded sense of time, and without the ritual of meals, classes, or meetings, I quickly learned about the desperate human need for structure.

In order to fend off the boredom and forget the fact of my solitude, I created structure for myself. Though I'd brought in with me a pair of *tefillin* so I could at least feel there was some Jewish content to the vision quest, I wasn't yet able to make use of them. I took hikes. I wrote poetry. I did anything I could to avoid being with myself. Yet when dusk arrived and even writing in my journal became an impossibility, I had no other choice but to acknowledge myself. I was alone. But I was alive. I'd entered the borderland. Nothing since has been as silent as that first night in the woods. Yet it was a silence as swollen with life as the darkness around me.

On my last day I decided to visit the Cliffs, about a three-hour hike in each direction. The minute I stepped onto the trail I started to cry. I'm not quite sure what triggered the tears—and I'm not really certain as to what kind of tears they were. Tears of loss, that's for sure. But also tears of acknowledgment. As if the wilderness were confirming my finitude, telling me that my humanity wasn't something I needed to avoid. With this knowledge that my past was dead and that the future was beyond my power to control, I began the ascent.

The cliffs themselves were barren, and the winds that gusted over them chilled me. From that vantage point, I had a 360-degree view of the region; it looked like a great green blanket, and, if I didn't know that within it were trails and roads, I'd have doubted that human civilization had ever touched it. The clouds rolled over the cliffs in caricatures, the sun pressing their shadows into the soil below. Two hawks soared past me. Then two more. Soon I saw half a dozen of them, leaping from ledge to ledge, gliding with the updrafts into the sky. I sat on a boulder and watched them for what must have been hours. I couldn't move. I was too much at peace.

I made it back to my tarp just as dusk began to set in. The woods darkened. I took out a candle from my backpack and stuck it in the ground. I'd done nothing in the last three days, no activities, no regimentation. That was what made it so difficult. I'd stripped myself bare and stared into the face of my own desolation. Now I was ready to return to the world, to the routines and rituals—even Jewish rituals—that in my sadness had seemed so pointless. I lit the candle. And I remembered the words of Rabbi Nachman of Bratslav, who observed, "No heart is as whole as the heart that has been broken."

The morning was cold. Yet for the first time in weeks, the first words out of my mouth formed a prayer: *Elohai, neshamah shenatatah bi tehorah hi* . . . "My God, the soul You have given me is a pure one." The wilderness, like a *mikveh*, had enveloped me, cleansed me. I took out my *tefillin*, an old, beaten pair that had once belonged to my grandfather and that had been given to me shortly after his death two years before. I wrapped the cracked leather straps around my left biceps and adjusted the headpiece over my forehead. I felt safe, as if I were being held by my grandfather's arms. I said the morning prayers. And I wondered: Was I over her? *Really* over her? I doubted it. But I could pray again. I could at least do that.

Conclusion

Reason, custom, peer pressure, guilt—none of these will ultimately convince today's Jews to observe the various mitzvot. There is no set rule any longer. Each of us will respond to Jewish rituals in different ways. What matters in a postmodern world is our personal, even existential, relationships with them. I've tried to show how Shabbat candles, Passover matzah, immersion in a *mikveh*, and laying *tefillin* have enhanced my own spiritual life, and how, at their best, mitzvot can serve as vehicles for sacred experience. I have depicted only four of them. There are 613 mitzvot to choose from.

In the sixteenth century, a rabbi and kabbalist named Isaac Luria developed a mystical system that has much to teach us today. Luria claimed that at the moment of creation, there was a kind of primeval Big Bang, a breaking of what he called the divine "vessels." As a consequence of this violent event, countless "sparks" were released from inside the vessels, filling every corner of the universe and all of human experience with latent spiritual power. Our task, argued Luria, was to gather up these sparks, a messianic undertaking, but one that would ultimately return the cosmos to its original state of harmony. The way to gather the sparks was through the performance of Judaism's many mitzvot.

While most of us today might not subscribe to Luria's worldview as a whole, his central message is clear: The mitzvot are our pathways to the sacred, our vehicles for achieving and experiencing spiritual encounter. They are the cornerstones of our Jewish lives. It may be the task of different Jews to "gather" different sparks, but it is as a people that we are accountable. The vast majority of American Jews do not believe that the mitzvot are divine creations and that our observance of them is God's literal will. How, then, do we persuade Jews to practice Jewish rituals? Not by arguing that they come from God, but that they can *lead* to God. The mitzvot are our people's response to God's reality, our link between the human and the divine, the finite and the infinite. They are our gateway to inner redemption.

In an age when those around us pray with crystals and worship trees, it is comforting to know that an ancient and beautiful collection of authentically Jewish rituals is ours just for the asking. Not all of us will have to enter the wilderness in order to discover this wonderful truth. Each of us has a unique path, and no one will respond to the same mitzvot in exactly the same way. But, with so much to gain, ignorance is unacceptable. We must be open to the power of mitzvot before they will work; we must invite God into our lives before God can enter.

The Torah reminds us that life is a gift, something we can either accept or reject. Yet God, through the mouth of Moses, makes it clear which alternative is the better one: "Choose life, therefore, that you and your descendents may live" (Deut. 30:19). If the mitzvot, as I've tried to demonstrate, are the very lifeblood of our Jewish souls, I would urge all of us to choose them as well.

The Four Questions
of Reform Jewish Life

E L Y S E   G O L D S T E I N

I was a Reform "poster child." I was a graduate of UAHC camps, in which I participated from early childhood through my late twenties, and NFTY activities, including a term as national vice president, and I continued the natural progression to Hebrew Union College. I always felt at home within the Reform movement. At the same time, I was becoming increasingly observant while still in high school and even more so during my university years at Brandeis. While I had never accepted the Orthodox notion of the divine authorship and infallibility of the Torah, Torah mi-Sinai, I felt drawn to observe Shabbat more fully, keep *kashrut*, pray with *tallit* and *kipa*. I lived for several years within the traditional community, becoming fully *shomeret Shabbat*, drawn to the mitzvot, including *mikveh*. I traveled between the Conservative movement, the "traditional egalitarian" *minyanim*, and the Orthodox world of *ba'ale teshuvah*, the newly observant (many of whom had been NFTY kids like me). My "home" of Reform sometimes seemed spiritually adrift, unanchored to any obvious set of expectations, with no clear codes or guides for ritual behavior and no defined belief system. My traditionally observant friends lived and breathed Judaism. It didn't go away on Saturday at four in the afternoon. They stopped what they were doing in the middle of a party to *daven Mincha*. They weren't upset about missing a concert if it fell on Shemini Atzeret. I envied them their certainty as well as their self-confidence about being Jewish. I longed for such passion among my Reform friends. Sure, I found it in the handful of us who kept coming back to camp until we were unit heads, who dance-led and song-led our way through college. Almost all of us talked about becoming rabbis, cantors, or Jewish educators. We "best and brightest" were drawn not only to tradition but also to learning. There were at that time no Reform Kolel programs, no liberal versions of such outreach study programs as the popular Aish ha-Torah or the Diaspora Yeshiva, the Jerusalem *ba'al teshuvah* haven, for us to "ascend" to. It seemed our limited choices as observant, serious, Torah-learning Reform Jews were either to become permanent *ba'ale teshuvah*—and thus leave the Reform movement for the Orthodox one—or to become Reform rabbis. So many of us felt conflicted. We felt let down by the very movement that had brought us to our passion for Judaism.

Ultimately it was my feminism that brought me back to identify with Reform Judaism. My feminism was a symbol of so much more: the ideas of personal autonomy, freedom of choice, evolving definitions of God and ongoing revelation coupled with actively seeking to translate those ideas into a Jewish life of true religiosity.

I knew all along that I wanted to be a rabbi, and it seemed appropriate to do so in the Reform movement, the place that supported my absolute, unequivocal right to pursue that path. So I returned. My level of personal observance seemed fine in light of the burgeoning interest in and acceptance of tradition at HUC in those years, the late '70s and early '80s. Many of my classmates kept kosher. Some students increased their Shabbat observances. A large number wore *tallit* and *kipa* and even *tefillin*. I was hardly alone. But I never managed—and still haven't managed—to solve that paradox of living within the movement philosophically while on the edges of the movement ritually.

Here I would like to take the role of the four children of the Passover haggadah who pose rhetorical questions in the guise of seeming innocence. They are categorized as wise, wicked, simple, and naive based on their question. My four questions are about the nature of Reform religious life. Each one can also be categorized, and with it, this author.

The first question I pose as the wicked child of the haggadah, who breaks off from the community: "How can I fit into a movement of choice when I have chosen to observe many mitzvot that other colleagues and laypeople do not observe?"

A story to illustrate. For many years, when I was a congregational rabbi, I accompanied the confirmation class on an intercongregational tour of Jewish New York. Each year we would stop one evening at a fast-food restaurant, where a colleague would ceremoniously and publicly order shrimp. He would eat it while sitting at the table with the confirmands. It always provoked great discussions late into the night, not only among the kids, but among the rabbis. It was definitely the "hot" point of the trip, but I always felt depressed at this moment. It seemed so awkward that this was the scene the confirmands always remembered, after half a year of discussing what it meant to live a Jewish life and a life of commitment to mitzvot.

I generally feel like the most religious one on the block. I'm shocked at how few of my colleagues choose to *daven* at CCAR conventions. I'm equally surprised at how traditional, how filled with Hebrew and singing those services are, compared to services at the congregations in which we serve. It is almost as if we've decided that we are not going to pray when we don't "have to," but when we do, we want it to be more traditional than our home services ever could be. I've never quite understood the contradiction.

Sometimes I grow tired of defending Reform Jews who practice little, care less, and demand much. Sometimes I grow weary of justifying why I am so much more observant than the average Reform Jew. Sometimes I don't want to be identified as the right wing of the movement. I'd like to see the center be totally committed to mitzvot, too.

The second question is a philosophical one. I ask this question as a theist who puts God in the center of the mitzvot, while still a Reform Jew who does not accept Torah as the literal word of God. I wonder what role God plays in the Reform conception of mitzvot. If we talk about Torah as God's word, then we ought to be following all of it. If we do not talk about Torah as God's word, then what is it to us? I perceive this as the question of the wise child, who desires enough information to count himself or herself in.

I am proud that the Reform movement is once again talking about God. I grew up in a Reform Judaism that revolved around freedom rides and anti-Vietnam marches, youth group bowling trips and sisterhood bake sales. The Jewish curriculum in Union camps in those days consisted of old-fashioned Hebrew-school-type Hebrew lessons—I can still remember morning classes in the old "formal gardens" at the UAHC Eisner Camp in Great Barrington—and Shabbat services in the outdoor sanctuary. We almost never spoke of God and most certainly never talked about mitzvot or religious obligation. When I returned home from the elitist Hebrew-speaking text study of Torah Corps in 1972 and wanted desperately to pray more in Hebrew, I was branded as a troublemaker in my temple.

So I am delighted when our biennials have workshops on God and mitzvot; when the CCAR publishes more ritual guides and fuller Siddurim. But my lifelong question about the place of God in our observance has yet to be answered. If the Torah is not literally God's will and God's word, then it is great literature, and the Jewish diary to be sure, but it does not have to hold me any more than any other great literature. But if it does contain God's will and God's word, then I better take it a lot more seriously! Why do I do some of God's will and not all of it? How do I know what is God's word and what is not? I feel sure that God does not want us to stone homosexuals and really doesn't care whether or not we mix wool with linen. I feel equally sure that *kashrut* is part of God's plan and so is Shabbat. How do I differentiate? Is God's word just the things I like? Just the things that resonate with the political consciousness of the day? We have made God's will those mitzvot we like, and those we don't we cast aside as relics of a patriarchal, primitive tribe. Sometimes it seems to me that the mitzvot that fall into the category of "God's will" are the ones we are able to "midrashize": They are the ones we can use to teach spiritual lessons in adult education around the festivals, or compassion to animals, or Shabbat. The ones for which we cannot find '90s spiritual vocabulary are discarded as "clearly" human adaptations or societal biases. Where is God in all of this? Did God speak at Sinai truly, metaphorically, or not at all?

The third question is a simple one, so it belongs to the simple child. How can I be such a right-wing Reform Jew in terms of ritual observance and yet remain so squarely in the left wing when it comes to political issues such as liturgical change for genderless worship? Many of us in the more right-wing camp of the CCAR find ourselves struggling to integrate these two ways of being, so we may call for more stringent boundaries regarding the role of the non-Jew in our synagogues, for example, while we also call for more relaxed boundaries regarding the role of homosexuals.

A story to illustrate. A few years ago, the editor of a conservative religious journal set about to identify the more "traditional" leaders of the Reform movement in an attempt to forge a kind of "return to values" group. Many of those who had expressed interest in the early Reform Roundtable discussions were called. A proto-statement was put forth for examination. On the surface, it had all the "right" issues: increased Hebrew in services, stricter observance of Shabbat and festivals, limiting ritual and liturgical roles for non-Jews in the synagogue, and the like. Further in, it linked concern on those fronts with assumed concern for the laxity of the Reform movement on other issues, specifically the emerging positive public role of homosexuals and changes in the liturgy to reflect gender sensitivity. The editor of the statement simply assumed that those on the right wing of the "mitzvot movement" would also find themselves against the ordination of homosexuals and against changes in the liturgy forced by the "fad" of feminism. Someone noticed there were not yet any women involved in this small group, and I was called. I quickly asserted my repugnance at the erroneous political implications of being religiously conservative.

So I live on the right wing of the movement at some times and the left wing at other times, and that is a precarious place to be, one of constantly changing allies and uncomfortable temporary coalitions.

The fourth question is from the child who does not know how to ask. It involves a discussion of feminist theory, and because much of it has not yet been asked at all, it waits on the side like the haggadah's fourth child, hesitating until he or she knows the right questions. Into the analysis of God as commander and we as the commanded I would like to see our movement consider a whole new set of references suggested by thinkers such as Judith Plaskow and Carol Gilligan. These feminist writers ask us to reconsider not only the nature of commandment but the entire notion of the role of law, and specifically in Judaism the mitzvot. Inherent in the system of mitzvot, and in all our discussions in the Reform movement so far about the "return to observance," lies the assumption that a system of rules—for us, the mitzvot—is by definition good. These discussions also assume that by "mitzvot"—whether we speak in a Reform context or otherwise—we mean "rules." The feminist critique challenges the previously unchallenged notion of patriarchy and hierarchy contained in the structure of all systems of rules. Such a critique does not suppose only that a certain law or laws are unjust or sexist. Instead, it supposes that the very idea of the need to govern by rules, the very notion of God as ruler and we as servants following that ruler's rules is a male way of ordering the universe.

Years ago Carol Gilligan wrote about the differences in the behavioral development of young girls and boys. Her book, *In a Different Voice*, posited that in general boys grow up attached to rules, and girls grow up attached to relationships. She noted how in boys' games, even in the closest-knit teams of boys, the policies and procedures are primary. If a player does not like the rules or abide by them, that player is simply off the field and the game goes on. But in girls' games, the relationships tended to be primary. If a girl did not like a particular game, the game would be changed rather than have the girl leave it. If a player did not want to follow the rules the other girls had established, the girls tended to change or alter those rules so as not to risk losing the player.

Thus Jewish feminists argue that the notion of "following the rules" in Judaism—that is, following the mitzvot—is a male way of defining Jewish behavior. Is it possible to see the mitzvot as something other than rules? I favor a relationship-based attraction to mitzvot, seeing mitzvot as "connectors" to both God and community rather than as regulations for which there is reward and punishment.

On another level, a feminist analysis of mitzvot will also open up the discussion of what I call the "theology of separation." Much of Jewish theology is based on *havdalot*—on making separations. The Saturday evening service separating Shabbat from the weekdays is a symbol of a deep and abiding concept at the heart of Jewish spirituality: that all things are essentially alike and yet different. Shabbat would not be special if it were like other days; *sukkot* would not be unique if we lived in them all the time. Heterosexual chemistry would not be possible if men and women were the same. The genius of Jewish spirituality is that it recognizes dualities all around us. Those differences are codified and clear: Shabbat/weekday, male/female, milk/meat, Jew/non-Jew, Israel/other nations, et cetera.

On the one hand, we recognize that something of the specialness of life is in marking these differences and in celebrating them. On the other hand, the centrality of separation speaks to a kind of independence not generally organic to women. Women are taught from early childhood to be bonded, to keep the family together, to rely on relationship. Women find great meaning in integration rather than separation, in wholeness rather than fragmentation, in interdependence rather than independence. Women seek fusion while men seek autonomy. Whether all this is "nature or nurture" we do not seem to know yet. But *halachah* in some measure is about keeping the lines solidly drawn between categories of being. What does that way of ordering the universe mean for women?

The rabbis teach that there are four levels of understanding Torah—*pshat, drash, remez,* and *sod*—meaning simple or literal, interpretive, the deeper possibility, and the mystical or hidden meaning.

On the *pshat* level live the literalists. What the Torah says, it means. The bottom line is: What you see is what you get.

Most Reform Jews, indeed many Reform rabbis, seem much more comfortable on the *drash* level. I love the powerful *midrashim* that we use, and in modern times we invent, to draw people in to do this mitzvah or that. We have created powerful new meanings for old ways; new metaphors for old images. But I have a memory of a time when I lived in a world of *pshat,* when the way seemed easy and straightforward and didn't have to be "midrashized." I see the powerful potential for *drash* in every mitzvah, but sometimes I long for a *pshat* answer. I don't always want to look long and hard to find more "suitable" answers, more "accessible" transliterations, adaptations, and abridgements of tradition that can be offered to the unwilling or reluctant. I admit that sometimes, just sometimes, I am jealous of my friends who did not go into the rabbinate after being "turned on" at NFTY or camp but who became *ba'ale teshuvah.* I see them and sometimes, in the recesses of my heart, I envy them the comfort of the occasional "I do it because it's *gescribben*—because it's written that you have to."

A Voice in the Dark:
How Do We Hear God?

ELYSE D. FRISHMAN

A profound theological struggle that liberal Jews have is to balance being commanded with having autonomy. When we use the language of mitzvah, we contradict ourselves; either we are commanded or we are not commanded. We appear to be petulant adolescents: "God, I know you want me to do this, but I don't want to."

There is an old cartoon where a minister is annoyed with his flock and says to them, "They are not the Ten Suggestions!" Well perhaps they are. Indeed, perhaps the entire halachic body of mitzvot are actually guidelines, rather than orders, offered by God.

Covenant can be understood in two ways: as obligation and as relationship. If one has little sense of relationship, covenant feels like a burdensome obligation. When one is embraced in relationship, the responsibilities of upholding it seem reasonable and necessary.

What happens when we don't feel commanded? Are we standing outside of the Jewish covenant with God? Is it possible to reinterpret the idea of mitzvah as something important but not commanded? And why would we observe mitzvot if they are not commandments from God?

Reform Judaism is based on voluntary covenant: We choose to live Jewishly. It is still crucial to base our theology in Torah. Torah is the starting point in all things Jewish. No matter what an individual believes, if it's not rooted in Torah, it's not Jewish; it is merely personal opinion. Torah has been commented upon, interpreted, even challenged; but all Judaism grows from it.

When we listen to Torah, we are listening to God's voice. But this is not necessarily what God speaks; it reflects what we hear. Dialogue between two people grows not from what is said but from what is heard. Consider the conversation between a teenager and parent. The child may hear the parent speaking in a certain tone and answer accordingly, while the parent is unaware of that tone. A student thinks the teacher is yelling at him, when the teacher is simply correcting. How often are we misunderstood because someone has misread our tone or style of speaking? Is it possible that one could interpret God's voice differently from the way it had been previously interpreted?

Tradition holds that God gave us mitzvot, that God commands certain behaviors. These commands were given in the Torah. We consider the dialogue of Torah as God speaking to us. But, what if, instead, we consider that the language of Torah is not necessarily God's; it's a record of how we heard God.

It is possible to reinterpret Torah according to this observation. There is no way to prove that God spoke these words. Even the fifteenth-century commentator Abravanel notes (in his commentary on *Parashat Bemidbar*) that the Torah isn't completely divine in origin; while God wrote the *halachah* of Torah, Moses wrote the *aggadah*. In the final analysis, we can't possibly know what God actually said. We can say definitively: This is how we heard God's voice. This is what has been recorded, as a result of our hearing.

How do we hear God's voice? And how does the Torah reflect what we and our ancestors have heard? Is it possible that reviewing mitzvot in Torah will reveal that they are not commandments? That they really are, as the old cartoon tries to say, suggestions?

Deborah Tannen, author of *You Just Don't Understand* and *Gender Discourse*, has observed that men and women communicate differently.

> Girls don't give orders; they express their preferences as suggestions and suggestions that are likely to be accepted. . . .
>
> Another researcher, Marjorie Harness Goodwin, compared boys and girls in two task-oriented activities. . . . She found that the boys' group was hierarchical: The leader told the others what to do and how to do it. The girls' group was egalitarian; everyone made suggestions and tended to accept the suggestions of others. However, observing the girls in a different activity—playing house—Goodwin found that they, too, adopted hierarchical structures. This study shows that girls know how to issue orders and operate

in a hierarchical structure, but they don't find that mode of behavior appropriate when they engage in task activities with their peers. . . . The chief commodity that is bartered in the boys' hierarchical world is status and the way to achieve and maintain status is to give orders and get others to follow them. . . . These dynamics are not the ones that drive girls' play. The chief commodity that is bartered in girls' community is intimacy."[1]

Tannen's work reveals that men listen for the sound of authority and respond to it. Men tell others what they want and expect them to obey. Women work for consensus, even women in positions of authority. While men view that as manipulative, women regard it as positive. Tannen records numerous conversations. Men appreciate status, women appreciate intimacy.

Torah has been interpreted traditionally by and for men. As more and more women are engaged in Torah study and commentary, a different interpretation can emerge, one that hears God not as Commander but as Partner.

We long for spiritual intimacy. American Jews in the late twentieth century are seekers, searching for their place in the cosmos. As American culture shifts, so do liberal Jewish needs. Previously successful models of congregational life no longer hold the same degree of effectiveness. The culture of our congregations is becoming less corporate and more spiritual. Reform Jewish worship is evolving from being formal, passive, and leader-centered to being highly interactive and congregant-centered. The idea of rabbi as autocrat is far less appealing than rabbi as facilitator, as one who enables others to live Jewishly. The language of the contemporary liberal synagogue must include the three Es: enabling, empowering, and embracing.

The eminent anthropologist Clifford Geertz suggests that each culture has its master story, which illustrates its values and direction. Lawrence Hoffman, in a class lecture, observed that for Jews, the master story is the Exodus from Egypt. We were freed from Egypt and slavery to become servants of God. Not to become self-fulfilled human beings but to become a people linked to God. God freed us from slavery—a time of no identity and no connection—in order to bring us into community and relationship. Its conclusion is that we are God's ser-

---

1: Deborah Tannen, *You Just Don't Understand (New York: Morrow, 1990)*, 44, 46–47.

vants, brought out from human slavery in order to serve God. In time, we came to God's mountain, Mount Sinai, to receive the words of Torah. As Moses related God's teaching to us, our people cried out, *"Na'aseh v'nishma!* We will do it and we will understand."* We linked ourselves in covenant with God.

Passover has been our most important holiday for centuries because it reenacted the master story. It also gave us a chance to wrestle with its message. And we did it with family, solidly binding family, God, and covenant together. But over time, our faith has corroded; we barely affirm the miracle at the Sea of Reeds. The ritual of Passover became more a celebration of universal freedom and the power of humans to effect this. Gone from many seders is that sense of connection to God. Some families use haggadahs that link the Exodus to the civil rights movement or the feminist struggle or survival despite the Holocaust. Ecology, human rights, personal identity have become the new symbols of freedom. All these causes are important—but how Jewish? And what about those that don't use a haggadah, or use one in Hebrew that no one but the leader can understand? The Jewish content is lost—and "Jewish" becomes synonymous with "being with family." It is no different than any grand family meal gathering.

To such Jews, the idea of being commanded by God simply holds no meaning. Even for observant liberal Jews, the language of mitzvah is a challenge. Do we hear God as Commander and ignore God? Or do we hear God communicating with us in a different way?

I will argue that there is more than one significant Jewish way to hear and experience God's voice. God communicates with us in Torah in three ways: speaking, saying, and commanding:

We hear God *speaking* to us in such phrases as: *"Vaydaber* Adonai el Moshe. . . . God spoke to Moses."

We hear God *saying* something to us: "Vaydabeir Adonai el Moshe *lemor.* . . . God spoke to Moses, saying."

We hear God *commanding* us: "Ka'asher *tzivah* Adonai el Moshe. . . . . As God commanded Moses."

These are the only three verbal forms of communication between us and God. Now let us consider the impact and content of each. There is a marked difference between a relationship that is commanded (hierarchical) and one that suggests give-and-take, reflecting a dialogue. Two of our verbs, *daber* (speak*)* and *amar* (say), are relational: God is talking with us. *Tzivah* (command) is hierarchical: God is commanding us. In

Torah, God is never interrupted in the *tzivah* form; but God is interrupted and even challenged in the *daber* and *amar* forms. One might ask if there is a significant difference between "speaking" and "saying." Indeed, "speak" has a formal connotation and is used throughout Torah to focus attention in a serious manner. "Say" is often more casual and general. Speech can be forceful; but there is a marked difference between employing the verb "command" or the verb "speak."

When are these different verbs employed? One would think that, considering the weight of the mitzvah system, *tzivah* would be the most important and most frequently used verb. We should be able to find it in all situations where important instructions or mitzvot are given.

The first specifically Jewish mitzvah is circumcision (Genesis 17:9–10, 22–23):

> God further said *(vayomer)* to Abraham: As for you, you and your offspring to come throughout the ages shall keep My covenant . . . every male among you shall be circumcised. . . . And when He was done speaking *(l'daber)* with him, God was gone from Abraham. Then Abraham circumcised the flesh of their foreskins on that very day, as God had spoken *(diber)* to him.

God does not command Abraham to circumcise. God is strongly directive; one might argue that Abraham was compelled by the tone of God's voice to comply. Consider instead: Perhaps Abraham feels moved to observe God's word because of their powerful bond. When God finishes speaking with Abraham, God's Presence departs. Abraham immediately observes the ritual—in order to draw close to God again. *Devekut*, bonding with God, could be regained through the act of circumcision.

The Ten Commandments are truly *Aseret ha-Dibrot*, literally, "the Ten Statements." Note the beginning of Exodus 20: "*Vaydaber* Elohim et kol had'varim ha'eleh *lemor*. . . . God spoke all these words saying." These verbs suggest that God isn't commanding; God is guiding, instructing, and relating to us.

The Holiness Code from Leviticus 19 contains crucial ethical and ritual instructions for Jewish living:

Vaydaber Adonai el Moshe *lemor,*
Daber el b'nei Yisrael, v'amarta alehem,
Kedoshim tih'yu ki kadosh ani. . . .

God spoke to Moses, saying,
Speak to the Children of Israel and say to them,
You shall be holy for I am holy. . . .

Abiding by God's words draws us closer to God; we don't need to be commanded to appreciate this. In fact, the commanding voice inhibits this. Ordering someone may accomplish the deed but won't enhance the relationship; it will further the distance. Dialogue, though, opens us to the possibility of being like God: *kadosh,* holy.

Similarly in the teaching of *kashru*t, the dietary laws, in Leviticus 11, the verb *tzivah* is not used:

Vaydaber Adonai el Moshe v'el Aharon *lemor* alehem,
Dabru el b'nei Yisrael *lemor,*
Zot ha'chayah asher toch'lu mi-kol ha-behemah asher al-ha'aretz.

Adonai *spoke* to Moses and Aaron, *saying* to them,
Speak to the Children of Israel, *saying,*
These are the animals that you may eat from among all the beasts on earth.

Whenever God addresses our people in Torah about something significant, God speaks with us. God is not demanding something; God is saying to us, "You want to be in relationship with Me? Here's how it works. . . . "I am reminded of Tannen's recordings of conversations between women. "These are my suggestions. I'd like, even expect, you to do them."

Is it possible that since we were slaves in Egypt that God thought we would be good slaves for God? That being used to taking orders in Egypt or suffering terrible consequences, we'd be pliant and obedient? No, God redeems us from mindless, cruel slavery! God wants us to observe; but the purpose is not to fulfill God's selfish needs. In contrast to Pharaoh, God's needs mirror our own. What's good for God is good for us.

Over the centuries, Jewish leaders have attributed suffering to nonobservance. For centuries, we've accepted the destruction of the Temples as a punishment from God for our noncompliance with mitzvot. I recall reading an article in an Israeli newspaper less than fifteen years ago about an Orthodox village suffering a series of bizarre catastrophes. The local rabbi ruled that this was a punishment because the women were not properly observing the laws of *niddah,* of ritual purity. This cause-and-effect attitude is hierarchical and controlling, and not at all what liberal Judaism professes. It belies the Holocaust and the myriad other catastrophes we've suffered. Abusive punishment is good for no one.

So why follow God's directions? Because they are compelling and infuse our lives with meaning. This is why liberal Jews observe and uphold the ritual and ethical guidelines.

Now, where in the Torah do we find the verb *tzivah?* It has both human and divine usage. It is used between people, such as when Rebecca commands Jacob to listen to her, and Isaac commands Jacob not to marry a Canaanite woman. The intent is to control: Do what I say without questioning! When men and women speak with one another in a clearly controlling manner, *tzivah* is the verb of choice.

Where in the Torah does God command? It is often found as a "tag line": "as God commanded. . . . " For example, this occurs after Abraham observes circumcision, "as God commanded." But God did not command circumcision. Interpret this as Abraham's perception of God's voice and authority: "as Abraham heard God commanding. . . ." Indeed, in every instance where this phrase is employed, this interpretation is possible.

Tannen teaches us that this is how men listen or hear. It says nothing about God's intended communication. One could argue that God would know that men would hear in this fashion and intended it so. Or one could argue that Torah is an eternal document: Whatever difficulties appear in the text reflect the concerns of the reader. Scholars of biblical criticism in nineteenth-century Germany tackled the discrepancy of animals on Noah's ark. In Genesis 6: 19ff., Noah is instructed to bring "of all that lives, of all flesh, two of each, male and female." In 7:2, God's instructions are different: "Of every clean animal you shall take seven pairs, males and their mates, and of every animal that is not clean, two, a male and its mate." The German scholars applied history and archeology to solve their dilemma, determining that authors with different agendas composed the diverse texts. Centuries earlier, rabbinic commentators arduously worked to reconcile such problems as "the Canaanites were then in the land." The word "then" implies a reflection on a past story. This challenged their theology that the Torah was written by God and given to Moses; since the Canaanites were indeed living in the land during Moses' lifetime, this expression appears to deny it. So who wrote the Torah? They solved the dilemma applying their own world perspective, concluding that "there is no before or after in the Torah."

The gift of our time is the insight of the social sciences: sociology, psychology, anthropology. We bring a new perspective to our most sacred text. Torah is the record of how we heard God's voice; now let us concentrate on the bias of the listener. How interesting that one of our central prayers, which comes from Torah, is the *Shema*! "Listen, Israel!" Why do we have to listen so deeply? Because it is truly hard to hear and comprehend God's intent.

In Torah, whenever men and women are gathered together, God speaks to the assembly. There are no instances of God addressing the assembly with the word "command." Even at the moment of revelation, the term *tzivah* is not used.

> Moses went and repeated to the people all the words of Adonai and all the rules; and all the people answered with one voice, saying, "And the words, which Adonai has spoken, we will do!"
>
> (Exodus 24:3)

Four verses later we read: "Then he [Moses] took the record of the covenant and read it aloud to the people. And they said: 'All that Adonai has spoken, we will do and understand.'"

Our ancestral mothers and fathers affirmed their commitment to God's words. They did not hear God as a commander; they did hear God's voice addressing them, speaking with them, and they wanted to respond, to follow, and understand. These were moments of deep awe, even fear, but basically the people were moved to observe God's word. Although one talmudic *midrash* suggests that they finally accepted God's covenant because God threatened to drop a mountain on them, the Torah certainly doesn't say this. The profound, spiritual bond with God was sufficient motivation.

Why is this important? So many Jews, men and women, are disenfranchised and relate little, if at all, to the mitzvah system. Reform Judaism's brilliance has been in its sociological understanding of people and ability to mesh that appreciation with a meaningful Jewish life. We are Jewishly active because God's guidelines are compelling to us.

Many of us do not hear God commanding. How powerful to realize that not only is *tzivah* employed less that we might have thought, but it is never a primary verb in the most significant interactions between our ancestors and God. God addresses us in Torah primarily in relationship, not as Commander. What came to be known as a body of mitzvot were originally gifts, words to direct and guide our lives meaningfully and to draw us close to God and holiness.

But what could sustain this relationship? What could insure the continuity of the mystical bond such that we would choose to stay in relationship with God? Is this a theology only for the committed? It appears that, over time, our sages represented God's word through the hierarchical system of *halachah,* which implanted the deed without relying upon the mystical bond. This was eminently practical, although it is interesting to note that mysticism was espoused by some of our greatest rabbis. Hasidism's early appeal was its emphasis on God's love and each person's ability to cleave to God. The institutionalizing of religious ideas seems to lead to hierarchy of rules rather than expressions of intimacy.

What is our motivation to live Jewishly, to follow God, if we are not commanded? The danger of voluntary covenant is nonparticipation. We certainly face this. American Jews do not feel obligated to participate. Jews become involved when they are touched so deeply that they are compelled to respond. A trip to Israel ignites a spark of commitment. Substantive teaching and meaningful worship motivate deeper synagogue involvement and home observance. It is crucial that our spiritual lives be strong. The challenge of our generation is to renew the power of *avodah,* to serve God rather than merely ourselves, to revitalize worship and recognize its ability to motivate Jewish living. Study of sacred texts and application of those teachings draw us close to God. That study must be not academic but spiritual and intellectual, touching the mind of the soul. We apply these teachings when they ring true to us, when God's voice resonates clearly for us. Then we choose to live Jewishly.

Where is responsibility in this theology of meaning? It comes from the obligations of true relationship, as in a marriage. There are limits we agree to in the way we treat one another and also God. Some may be communally determined, such as when to observe Shabbat, but the how of observance is personally derived, like defining Shabbat rest.

Adopting the language of mitzvah is confusing. Mitzvah means "commandment." Certainly many think of mitzvah as a "good deed"; ethical mitzvot fall under this idea. But what of the ritual mitzvot? These are not necessarily ethical. Do we only do Jewish deeds that are ethical? Certainly not. Yet, the word *mitzvot* is actually misleading if we understand these to be guidelines rather than commandments. The language of our prayers is also misleading. Common blessings, such as for lighting Shabbat candles, include the formulaic line *asher kidshanu b'mitzvotav v'tzivanu*. . . who has sanctified us through commandments and commanded us to. . . . We have to be acrobats of theological language to reconcile this one. For a movement whose liturgical leaders removed *mechayeh metim* (God who revives the dead), one could expect a more thorough theological response to mitzvah blessings.

What is a liberal *ba'al teshuvah*, a Jew who is drawn deeply into liberal Jewish expression? One who embraces autonomy, yet is prepared to tackle spiritual issues. This wrestling inevitably draws one into ritual observances, as vehicles for deeper spiritual exploration. And with these ritual expressions come humility and expressions of compassion, the sense that "I am receiving so much; how can I give back?" By working in the soup kitchen, regularly adding to the food cupboard, participating in ongoing *tzedakah* projects. Obligation proceeds from a covenant of relationship.

Each generation of Jews faces a crisis of one sort or another; when it's not persecution, internal hypocrisies are self-destructive and require a good antidote of ethics (musar) or renewed joy and celebration of the human spirit (hasidut) or the popularizing of the mystical path (neo-hasidic) or the creative renewal of ritual (Reform). We have survived because we are creative and we want Judaism to survive. We love our faith. Being commanded may or may not have much to do with it.

Indeed, the desire for relationship motivates covenant participation. A favorite story about the bond between individual, community, and God comes from folk tradition about the Baal Shem Tov, known as the Besht, the founder of Hasidism.

The Besht and his disciples would *daven* together every morning. Shabbat was especially celebrated with schnapps and cake following worship. The wonderful aroma of the food would waft into the sanctuary, and stomachs would rumble; but no one could think of leaving until all were finished. The Baal Shem Tov, the Besht, would *daven* longer than anyone else. After the last disciple had finished, the Besht would be covered in his *tallit*, swaying intently back and forth. All would wait patiently until he had completed his journey.

But one morning before the rebbe arrived, a disciple whispered to the others, "You know, each week we wait until he is finished, and each week my stomach grumbles louder and louder with anticipation! What if we were to sneak away quietly and grab a bite, then hurry back in—he'd never notice, he's so immersed in his prayers." The others protested, but their appetites won over. That morning, as they watched the Besht sway and utter prayers beneath his *tallit*, they began to leave the sanctuary in utter silence. Suddenly, the Baal Shem Tov lifted up his head and found them.

"Where are you going?" he cried. With embarrassment, they confessed. "But how did you know we were leaving?" they asked. "We didn't make a sound!" He responded softly, "When I pray, it is as though there is a ladder stretching from earth to heaven, and I ascend that ladder. But you, you hold up the rungs. And when you left, I fell."

Connecting with God is also about building a spiritual community. Reaching for God, the rebbe needed his friends. So with you and me. Together, we reach higher.

We tend to think of our search as a solitary one, between an individual and God. Judaism suggests that the quest is shared. This is the meaning of covenant, a communal contract between us and God that each person fulfills. We learn this from the commandment for circumcision. God says: All that ignore this shall be cut off from their kin. Not from God, but from the community.

Perhaps the extensive comfort and security possessed by American Jewry frees us to hear God's voice differently from the way a persecuted community might. Indeed, freedom is our reality. The current trend toward spiritual life reflects a desire for more than personal fulfillment. We want to be part of something greater than our individual selves. We yearn for true community. We seek God. And God's voice need not be heard as stern and commanding. God is the blessed Holy One: loving, caring, and seeking relationship with us.

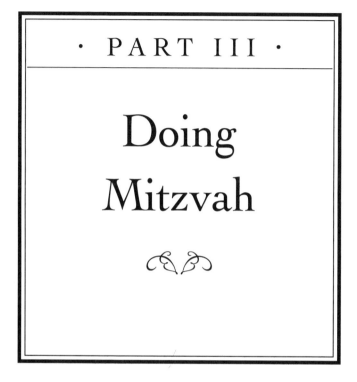

· PART III ·

Doing
Mitzvah

Re-creating the Narrative Community

or

It's Hard to Do Mitzvot by Yourself

PETER S. KNOBEL

> You stand this day, all of you, before the Lord your God—your
> tribal heads, your elders and your officials, all the men of Israel,
> your children, your wives, even the stranger within your camp,
> from woodchopper to waterdrawer—to enter into the covenant of
> the Lord your God, which the Lord your God is concluding with
> you this day, with its sanctions; to the end that He may establish
> you this day as His people and be your God, as He promised you
> and as He swore to your fathers, Abraham, Isaac, and Jacob. I
> make this covenant, with its sanctions, not with you alone, but
> both with those who are standing here with us this day before the
> Lord our God and with those who are not with us here this day.
>
> (Deuteronomy 29:9–14)

On Yom Kippur, we read these verses from Deuteronomy. They constitute the central assertion of the Jewish master story, which says that each Jew is included in the covenant at Sinai. Every Jew from top leadership down: those who performed unskilled but necessary labor; those who were physically present at the mountain when the covenant was proclaimed; and those who were not present, those who were not yet born are included in and stand obligated under the *b'rit*, the covenant. Our collective presence at Sinai is a criterion for inclusion in the community and allegiance to observance of the divine mandates (mitzvot) whose authority is rooted in that mythic moment. Theologically, it is God's drawing near to Israel in the thunder and lightning of revelation that transformed Pharaoh's slaves into God's servants. Through the mouth of Moses and all of his successors (female and male) we have tried to live out the implications of that moment.

The intimacy of Moses' relationship with God, which is reflected in our collective encounter, translates relationship into deeds—positive and negative commandments, doing and refraining from doing. Religious leadership has the primary task of creating deeds, ritual and ethical, that maintain the memory of the initial experience and create opportunities for its being reexperienced. The Passover seder and the lighting of the *chanukiah* are two prime examples. Through these actions we recall and reexperience the mighty acts of God and know how to live our life in response to them. It becomes a way of life crystallized into law, *halachah*, or in liberal terms a mitzvah system. For deeds to be effective in community building and creating a unique way of life, they need to be regularized and become the norms of the community. Our identification with this moment and its meaning in large measure determines how we live our Jewish lives.[1]

Further in the same passage in Deuteronomy we read:

> Surely, this mitzvah which I enjoin upon you this day is not too baffling for you, nor is it beyond reach. It is not in the heavens, that you should say, "Who among us can go up to the heavens and get it for us and impart it to us, that we may observe it?" Neither is it beyond the sea, that you should say, "Who among us can cross to the other side of the sea and get it for us and impart it to us, that we may observe it?" No, the thing is very close to you, in your mouth and in your heart, to observe it.
>
> (Deuteronomy 30:11–14)

Obligation is collective but accessible to each person. It is not the esoteric wisdom of the elite but the exoteric practice of the people. The key to participation is knowledge, and knowledge is available through study. The rabbis exercised authority based on expertise and in matters of dispute determined the law by majority vote. The most famous illustration of this comes from the Talmud:

1: The question of identification with the master story has significant implications for the way people live their lives. Lawrence Kushner's *Honey from a Rock* (New York: Harper and Row, 1977) is a successful attempt to identify biblical narratives with incidents in contemporary life. His goal is to help people discover the holy in the ordinary.

It has been taught: On that day R. Eliezer brought forward every imaginable argument, but they did not accept them. Said he to them: "If the *halachah* [law] agrees with me, let this carob tree prove it!" Thereupon the carob tree was torn a hundred cubits out of its place—others affirm, four hundred cubits. "No proof can be brought from a carob tree," they retorted. Again he said to them: "If the *halachah* agrees with me, let the stream of water prove it!" Whereupon the stream of water flowed backward. "No proof can be brought from a stream of water," they rejoined. Again he urged: "If the *halachah* agrees with me, let the walls of the school-house prove it," whereupon the walls inclined to fall. But R. Joshua rebuked them, saying: "When scholars are engaged in a halachic dispute, what right have you to interfere?" Hence they did not fall, in honor of R. Joshua, nor did they resume the upright, in honor of R. Eliezer; and they are still standing thus inclined. Again he said to them: "If the *halachah* agrees with me, let it be proved from heaven!" Whereupon a heavenly voice cried out: "Why do you dispute with R. Eliezer, seeing that in all matters the *halachah* agrees with him!" But R. Joshua arose and exclaimed: "It is not in heaven." What did he mean by this? — Said R. Jeremiah: That the Torah had already been given at Mount Sinai; we pay no attention to a heavenly voice, because You have long since written in the Torah at Mount Sinai: After the majority must one incline.

R. Nathan met Elijah and asked him: What did the Holy One, blessed be He, do in that hour?—He laughed [with joy], he replied, saying, "My children have defeated Me, My children have defeated Me."[2]

The passage is used to assert the authority of the rabbinic courts to determine the correct interpretation of the law. Human authority to interpret revelation wins out over appeals to special wisdom given to the individual directly by God. It means that each generation must interpret sacred texts to discover their implications and applicability to the present. It also means that the community in which a Jew resides determines how the mitzvot are to be observed.

One of the most interesting aspects of the talmudic passage is the

---

2: *Bava Metzia* 59b.

conversation between God and Elijah. It tells us that God wants us to work out the implications of revelation and apply them to real situations in our own lives. In Judaism religious living is the application of the human mind to the sacred texts in the light of political, social, and economic circumstances to sanctify the everyday. What a person does or refrains from doing is in large measure determined by the community in which a person locates himself/herself. By community I mean the effective community, namely, the one that a person considers his/her peer group. A person's behavior is in part regulated by the norms of that group. The loss of an effective Jewish community has meant a significant decline in observance and identification with a distinct way of living.

Our understanding of mitzvah is conditioned by the social situation in which we live, but it is also conditioned by the overarching question, What does God want us to do? An interesting example is derived from the observance of Shabbat. In Genesis 2:2–3 God rests, blesses, and hallows the seventh day, thereby creating Shabbat. Each week the Jew who observes Shabbat also rests, blesses, and hallows the day in order to create Shabbat. Without human action, Shabbat does not come. If we do not set this time aside, Friday night and Saturday remain Friday night and Saturday. They never become Shabbat. The time remains in the category of *chol* (ordinary) rather than *kadosh* (holy.) God may proclaim Shabbat and even observe it, but only if Jews imitate God does Shabbat exist as a reality in people's lives.

The vast majority of Reform Jews are not Shabbat observers in any meaningful way. I believe one major reason is because there is no social support for observing. The general culture does not support it. The secular concept of time does not include Friday night and Saturday in the category of holy or religious. A Jew who wishes to observe must make a countercultural decision, one that is made more difficult by the lack of social support and, to a certain extent, isolation when one's peer group is not observing.

A counter example is evident in the success of UJA/Federation in making support for Israel and for communal welfare a mitzvah for a significant number of Jews by creating peer groups who make membership in that peer group dependent upon the willingness of its members to participate by giving *tzedakah* and soliciting *tzedakah* from others. It has also used missions to Israel as a means of forming communities of common "religious" experience, which motivate ever-greater commitment. Participants often describe these missions as life changing. First-hand experience translates into more than intellectual assent. The emotive aspects of the experience are internalized. UJA/Federation then attempts to follow up on these experiences to translate them into deeds and maintain a sense of continued participation in a community of common experience.

Each religious stream has attempted to offer an approach to religious living that either affirms or denies that particular actions deemed mandatory by past generations are binding on us. The progressive movements have also discovered new obligations based on our changing knowledge base. When obligation coheres with our self-understanding, then mitzvah has a natural place in our lives. My personal experience with classical Reform Judaism and especially that aspect of it that is known as prophetic Judaism is a case in point. Classical Reform Judaism provided a sense of transcendent meaning to many in my generation (1950s and 1960s). It created and then validated our desire to create an ideal society as the "mission of Israel." The demands of liberal politics and liberal religion were in our view the same. Our peer group and our parents believed and acted on this assumption. Temple religion, especially on the occasion of the annual gathering of the community on the High Holy Days, reinforced this understanding. God did not care about ritual but demanded righteousness. Synagogue attendance was of secondary importance. *Kashrut* (the dietary laws) and *kipot* (head coverings) worked against our desire for a new universalistic age. We believed we were among the vanguard of those who would bring about the Messianic Age. Our reading of texts was selective and limited. The *Shema* taught us about the one God of all humankind. We read the Exodus from Egypt with its admonition that a society is judged by how it treats its weakest members. We read selections from the Prophets that criticized an oppressive establishment unconcerned about the welfare of the poor and hungry, and we repeated over and over the text from Isaiah as we sought to beat weapons of mass destruction into farm implements. Our concern was almost exclusively universal and in the post- World War II era it was coherent with the optimistic ideology of American culture. Our community and our culture defined mitzvah. I wish to emphasize that it gave meaning to our lives and it provided genuine Jewish content to our existence. While I now look back on it as inadequate, there is no denying that the experience made me a fervent Reform Jew.

That era has ended and we are now, in large measure, part of the narcissistic and solipsistic culture of the 1980s and 1990s although we can detect among a growing number a desire for spirituality. Some of this is merely a continuation of an individualistic therapeutic model for personal growth and well-being that was exemplified in books like *I'm Number One* and *I'm OK, You're OK*, but some of it is a genuine desire to find a religious community and a religious life that will engage Jews in significant human interactions that will be the locus for their feeling in relationship to God. Almost two decades ago the Central Conference of American Rabbis produced in turn *Gates of Mitzvah: A Guide to the Jewish Life Cycle* in which four distinguished Reform thinkers offered their own definition of the word *mitzvah*. But in the body of the book and its successor *Gates of the Seasons: A Guide to the Jewish Year*, the word *mitzvah* remained untranslated.[3] While this has been a useful strategy, it ultimately undermines the seriousness of the whole enterprise. For practical as well as ideological reasons, the Central Conference of American Rabbis could not offer a single theological understanding of the origin or authority of mitzvah. Yet in a real sense each of the authors concludes that there are deeds that are done in fulfillment of the divine will. Roland Gittelsohn defined mitzvah as living in conformity to the forces in the world that preserve and enhance human life. For him, those forces were God, and Judaism's collective wisdom told Jews how to live. While God's will for him was not transcendent but immanent in nature, doing what Judaism taught had divine authority, as he understood it. David Polish identified mitzvah as the result of the historic encounter between God and the Jewish people. Herman Schaalman emphasized God's commanding presence. Arthur Lelyveld limited the realm of divine interest to ethics but he had no doubt that God's demands for justice were clear and unequivocal. The decision not to translate the word *mitzvah* was designed to suggest a seriousness about action that went beyond the question of origin. Deed took precedence over creed. Theology was secondary to observance.

Mitzvot are deeds that Jews perform and acts from which we refrain in fulfillment of God's will. While this is a difficult and problematic statement, without at least an a priori commitment to the concept that

---

3: When this volume was written, no women were asked to contribute—something that would not happen today.

God makes demands upon us and that we are, no matter how imperfectly, able to know them, Judaism is reduced to a series of strictly human choices. To consider oneself to be in the service of God is what ultimately gives Judaism its meaning as a way of life and why it is worthy of being an exemplar to the rest of humankind and a force for redemption.

How can we re-create for ourselves the sense that doing mitzvot is of the utmost most importance? Doing mitzvot is more than building a Jewish identity: It is doing God's work. The feminist theologian Rachel Adler in her book *Engendering Judaism* describes her method of Torah study in the following manner:

> What is God telling us through this story? What are we telling God through this story? Having wrestled the story for a blessing, what meanings have we wrested from it? How does the story shape our collective memory as a people? What demands does it make upon us that we must integrate into the way we live our lives? How will we transmit the story?[4]

I believe she offers us an appropriate model for establishing significant Torah study communities that become mitzvah-doing communities. From such text study in community will emerge a serious new praxis. The following passage from the Mishnah that appears in our Siddur (prayer book) makes it clear that the key to knowing and doing mitzvot is derived from Torah study:

> These are duties whose worth cannot be measured:
> Honoring one's father and mother
> Acts of love and kindness
> Diligent pursuit of knowledge and wisdom
> Hospitality to strangers
> Visiting the sick
> Celebrating with bride and groom
> Consoling the bereaved

4: Rachel Adler, *Engendering Judaism* (Philadelphia:Jewish Publication Society of America, 1998), xxv.

Praying with sincerity
And making peace where there is strife
And the study of Torah leads to them all.[5]

As I have stated above, mitzvah is defined ultimately by the community in which one lives, and from a practical point of view it's very difficult to do mitzvot by yourself. I believe that people who see themselves as part of an observing community will observe mitzvot when they are alone, but few people will be able to develop a rich Jewish life by themselves. With the breakdown of family as the natural locus for observance, Jewish institutions (especially synagogues) will have to create communities of observance.

Every community possesses the master narrative, which tells its story and explains its values. Members of the community understand the story as their own and live out the story through ritual and ethical acts that are consistent with membership in the community. They discover in the texts incidents in their own life. The recovery of mitzvah in Reform Judaism requires the rebuilding of observant narrative communities—groups of worshiping, studying, and practicing Jews who identify the Jewish story as their own. The primary element in the Jewish story is the collective encounter with God, which is reexperienced in Torah study and mitzvah. Therefore mitzvah is a reenactment of an encounter with God as experienced by the community. Reform Judaism's overemphasis on personal autonomy and the individual as decision maker has undermined the support system necessary to "hear God's voice" calling us to holiness.

> The Eternal spoke to Moses, saying: Speak to the whole Israelite community and say to them: You shall be holy, for I, the Eternal your God, am holy.
>
> (Leviticus 19:1–2)

What is crucial in this text is the phrase "*kedoshim tiheyu*—you [plural] shall be holy." The command is addressed to the whole Israelite community. Holiness is understood as *imitatio dei*, imitating God. This means both in the ritual and ethical realm. God not only clothes the

---

5: *Gates of Prayer for Shabbat and Weekdays, (New York: Central Conference of American Rabbis, 1994),* 13.

naked and visits the sick but also observes Shabbat and prays. Therefore, what we do is important. Relationship with God is derived from behaving like God.

In Reform Judaism much emphasis is given to the individual as locus for decision-making. The spirit of the age as well as the North American context of the bulk of liberal Jews makes this appear correct and natural. Individual freedom, especially freedom from control of a religious community, is characteristic of the political landscape in which most Reform Jews live. Religion has been relegated from the public to the private realm. Society is officially neutral on religious behavior except where it is deemed dangerous to an individual or to the society as a whole. Religion is a voluntary act that cannot be coerced by the instrumentalities of the state or by the religious community itself against the will of the individual. Even membership in a synagogue does not require or prohibit specific behaviors once the monetary obligations have been fulfilled. Liberal theology has also removed another important coercive factor, namely, divine providence. There is neither reward nor punishment in this world or in the next.[6] All these were hard-won victories, but ironically they have left individuals isolated, without the necessary support to establish a meaningful Jewish life.

I wish to reemphasize that in Judaism, mitzvot derive from the communal encounter of God and humankind. Unique individuals such as Moses, Miriam, or Isaiah may have special insight that allowed them to help the community understand the divine mandates, but Sinai is a collective revelation geared to the capacity of each individual. Individuals in communities of observers observe mitzvot. The communities share a canon of authoritative texts the interpretation of which determines the boundaries of observance. In observant communities, *talmud torah* (Torah study) is a primary category of behavior because it provides authoritative ground for observance. We might describe these as textual communities. In other words, members of the community agree that certain texts are authoritative for belief and practice. The agreement is sometimes explicit and sometimes implicit. An urgent need in liberal Judaism is a discussion of the canon. What books and

---

6: Liberal versions of the afterlife concentrate either on naturalistic immortality, e.g., our lives have had an effect on this world, or on vague and metaphoric notions of the immortality of the soul.

individual texts constitute the canon and what are the criteria for their inclusion and exclusion? For example, in classical Reform Judaism all those texts that dealt with the dietary laws or laws of priestly purity were considered null and void. There were congregations that established unique Torah reading cycles that skipped those passages. Herman Cohen's neo-Kantian philosophical understanding of Judaism as a religion of reason became the lens through which we evaluated Judaism. Mystical texts such as the Zohar were dismissed as nonsense. Today these texts are being reevaluated. In addition, we now have a growing body of Jewish feminist literature that is for many of us authoritative.

The congregation is the most likely place for us to begin the process of the re-creation of the narrative community. Serious text study for adults must pervade every aspect of congregational life. Congregations should establish a goal of devoting as many resources to the education of adults as they do to the education of children. They should provide settings in which children and adults could study texts together and separately simultaneously. Text study should begin with the blessing for the study of Torah. Ideally, an element of communal worship should either precede or follow text study.[7] Strategically it is possible to create subgroups in existing congregations who will establish mini-covenants around groups of mitzvot: *tikkun olam* (social action), *tefillah* (prayer), *bikkur cholim* (visiting the sick), *talmud torah* (learning), et cetera. Each subgroup would study and do. More than three decades ago, Roland Gittelsohn introduced the idea of a *b'rit ketanah*, an individualized commitment to perform certain mitzvot. It has been introduced in a number of congregations with varying degrees of success. It is a marvelous idea because it offers an individual the opportunity to contemplate how he/she wishes to strengthen his/her personal Jewish life. It is usually limited in scope and therefore seems an ideal vehicle for making incremental change. The reason it is rarely more than minimally successful is because individuals do not live in isolation. They usually live in multiperson households and socialize with specific indi-

---

7: An urgent need is the restoration of daily worship. Synagogues should use opportunities when people are gathered to insure that communal worship is included. It will require significant effort, but high-quality, brief worship that is regularized affirms that whatever activity is taking place is part of doing God's business. The perfunctory prayer or the brief ("Keep it short, Rabbi") *devar Torah* is insufficient.

viduals or groups of individuals. Without including this familial and social network in the attempt to change one's pattern of observance, one is faced with either a lack of support or outright resistance. In this context, a supportive peer group becomes all the more important.

It should be of more than passing interest to note that when Jewish seekers visit a Chabad house or any synagogue that has an active program of encouraging minimally observant Jews to move toward Orthodoxy, they are provided instantly with a warm welcome and multiple invitations to join in communal activities. They are invited to share Shabbat in people's homes. They are provided with a mentor and integrated with other seekers. This provides a level of comfort and support and also an instant community. They experience observance as joyous service of God. Their lives take on new meaning. Many report that they have discovered that their lives have a purpose. While in the liberal community we may be concerned about some of the tactics in the *ba'alei teshuvah* movement, what is undeniable is that the newly observant find community and meaning. They are also engaged in vigorous learning taught by people who themselves are believers.

Talmud torah (Torah study) is not neutral academic learning but engaged learning whose goal is personal transformation and living a holy life. *Talmud torah* takes place in community. The Western academic model of frontal teaching and homework done in solitude is not the model of traditional Torah study. Learning in *Chavrutah* (in pairs or small groups) makes learning a social encounter that is described by rabbinic tradition as bringing the presence of God.

Congregations have existing groups that may be a starting point. First are congregational chavurot (groupings of members), which in many cases are small communities or, as they often describe themselves, extended families. Second is congregational leadership, especially the boards of trustees.[8] Committees can be transformed into learning and doing communities. Our efforts should be first with those who are open to increased Jewish practice and study. The goal of the

---

8: If the leadership of the synagogue is truly an observing community, I believe it will have a "trickle-down" effect on the synagogue. This is not accomplished by making rules for how many services board members must attend or what programs they must attend. The transformation takes place only if worship and study can be shown to improve the quality of the "business" of the synagogue and touch the members of the board in the process.

study ought to be explicit. While *talmud torah* (learning) for its own sake is a mitzvah and is an important component of any congregational education program, explicit practical Torah study is necessary for religious living. These emerging communities need a body of texts that will teach them about specific mitzvot, how they are to be performed, and their meaning. They should engage in the give-and-take of a talmudiclike argument to agree collectively on what they are going to do or not do. The group should vote, preserving the record of the vote and the arguments on each side. Members of the group should commit themselves to accepting the collective wisdom of the group. Decisions should come up for periodic review and in some cases a pluralism of behaviors would be deemed within the collective norm.

For example, in a group dealing with the observance of Shabbat, the lighting of the Shabbat candles is a mitzvah. The proper time for lighting might be either eighteen minutes before sunset, using darkness as a criterion, or when the household or the community gathers to welcome Shabbat, using a sociological definition for the beginning of Shabbat. More complex would be to determine what activities are permitted and what are prohibited. Definitions of work, *menuchah* (rest), *oneg* (joy), and *kedushah* (holiness) would require study and discussion. Are acts of *tikkun olam* (social action) that are not of an emergency nature permitted on Shabbat? What kinds of recreational activities meet the criteria established by *menuchah, oneg,* and *kedushah*? Is it possible for different individuals to consider the same acts permitted and prohibited on Shabbat? For example, gardening is prohibited for me on Shabbat because I find it to be work, but another individual may find an example of rest and communion with nature. In effect, the group would be developing an open code and establishing a pluralistic *halachah*. This would be a serious enterprise. It would draw congregants and rabbis, along with cantors, educators, and executive directors, closer together.

For example, a group that decided to concern itself with the issue of poverty, hunger, or homelessness would study relevant texts, look at existing programs that are aimed at alleviating these conditions, and evaluate them. A primary concern would be: Do they treat the poor with dignity and respect, as required by Torah? Do they properly respond to their needs? The group would then determine which existing programs to support and what new ones to devise. The group would develop ritual and prayer to accompany acts of *tzedakah* (the required concern for the poor) and *gemilut chasadim* (deeds of loving-kindness).[9]

Ultimately mitzvah is doing God's work as members of the Jewish people. The recovery of sacred duty and obligation is our primary task. Our goal is not the imposition of a code from a coercive communal authority but the rebuilding of a genuine relationship with God that will inspire Jews to wish to live out the implications of that relationship. God may be discovered in the unique encounters we have with nature or in lonely moments of self-encounter, but God is most frequently present in our relationships with others. It is communal prayer that teaches us the words to say when we are alone. It is communal study that helps us to determine what is right and what is wrong. In community we hold the hand of our neighbor and our neighbor can hold our hand. Weeping together makes the pain less bitter and laughing together makes the joy that much sweeter. Alone we can accomplish many things, but together we can repair the world.

Only when Jews allow ancient and modern sacred texts to form the basis for building a Jewish life can we speak a common sacred tongue. The language of autonomy will then be bankrupt beyond our rejection of the tyranny of others. If God is my friend and my beloved, my loving parent, the source of my being and the creator of the universe, then through learning and doing in community, I will discover how to bring my will into concert with the divine will. I know what my parents want before they command me. I know what I must do for my lover before she tells me. I understand what it means to live on property that is not my own. When I am confused and do not know the answer, I can turn to other people. Praying and studying together, we learn what God requires of us. Life is with people. God is with people. Mitzvah is with people. It is difficult to be Jewish alone. In Jewish living our "I" must become "we," for all of us stood at Sinai together.

9: Any such group would require support and resources from the congregation or from the Reform movement. A full curriculum should be available. Teachers, leaders, or facilitators must be trained. Activities such as *kallot* or *shabbatonim* are essential for community building. Any transformative activity requires a grest deal of work. This can happen only if the leadership or congregation and the movement agree upon the seriousness of the enterprise. If we see ourselves as a God-centered movement whose mission is to fulfill our obligations under the *b'rit*, the covenant, we can change what is to what ought to be. My optimistic attitude is a legacy from my having been raised in the Reform movement and having been taught that we can bring about the Messianic Age.

The Command to Study

ANDREW N. BACHMAN

It became a supreme commandment to "study," to explore the
Scriptures. It leaves many things open, it is full of questions; what
is merely suggested has to be followed to the end; passages that
appear to be contradictory have to be reconciled; and what is left
open has to be filled in. The Holy Scripture is the most stable element of Judaism and at the same time its most dynamic force.

Leo Baeck, *The Essence of Judaism*

Mitzvah is born in the terrifying and insecure moments of a soul's
reckoning of the world. In Judaism's most sublime moment, we encounter it at Sinai in the attempt to discern God's word and where, according to the legend, the newly liberated Jewish people were coerced
into accepting the yoke of the commandments under an overturned
mountain. To some Jews today, mitzvah connotes a coercive religious
system with antiquated requirements. To others, it has merged with
the bland notion of a "good deed." I would like to focus attention on
one mitzvah that has the capacity to renew our view of all the rest—
the command to study.

For all that has been said about the contemporary Jewish struggle
for identity and selfhood, I would argue that in the very process of
learning—or what the tradition calls *talmud torah*—we can find ourselves in relation to community and together encounter mitzvah, the
commanding voice of God. For students new to Judaism and Torah
study, the experience of understanding mitzvah begins with a question,
usually "why," and ends with the paradox of possibilities. With regard

to ritual, for example, we may ask why we light candles or why we say the blessing over bread. In the process of *talmud torah,* we discover that while the tradition commands these acts, the tradition also presents us with a variety of reasons for those actions, ultimately rooting them in the voice of God. As Jewish doers we are necessarily Jewish learners, since revelation, however we may understand it, is traditionally most firmly rooted in the moment God gave Torah to the Jewish people at Sinai. As Jewish learners, we are commanded to study, to know, and to seek out answers to the questions that may arise for us. For some the search is factual, such as the desire to know the characters and plots of biblical stories. For others, the experience of delving deeply into the pages of Torah by engaging in *talmud torah* reflects the desire to learn what Judaism and, ultimately, what God demand of us.

Given the imperative of *talmud torah,* it is surprising at the least that Reform Judaism, while historically asserting the value of continued education, has neglected the central notion of *talmud torah lishmah:* Torah study for its own sake. Indeed, it was not until the publication of *Gates of Prayer: The New Union Prayerbook*[1] that the mitzvah of *talmud torah,* mentioned in the *Birchot ha-Torah* (Torah Blessings) of the Morning Service, was restored to the prayer book and acknowledged in worship.[2] The specific phrase—*talmud torah k'neged kulam* (the study of Torah is equal to all mitzvot of action), taken from Mishnah—in a way overturns earlier Reform commitments: to prophetic Judaism as opposed to rabbinic Judaism, and to the realm of social action, which played such a dominant role in liberal conceptions of mitzvah. Returning to the prayer book this section of Mishnah—a legal code—functionally raises study to the level of a spiritual and legal commandment. The previous *Union Prayerbook,* Isaac Mayer Wise's *Minhag America,* and David Einhorn's *Olat Tamid* lack any reference to this prayer.[3] This is

---

1: *Gates of Prayer: The New Union Prayerbook (New York:* Central Conference of American Rabbis, 1975), 52-53.

2: Ibid. This prayer is found in *B.T. Shabbat* 127a and *Kiddushin* 39b, which are elaborations on the section from *Mishnah Peah* 1:1.

3: Both Michael Meyer in his *Response to Modernity* (New York: Central Conference of American Rabbis, 1977) and Chaim Stern and A. Stanley Dreyfus in their notes to Lawrence Hoffman's *Gates of Understanding* (New York: Oxford University Press, 1990) hint that the reason for early Reformers' reluctance to include this prayer is due to its association with the talmudic tradition. Early Reformers saw themselves as exemplars less of the rabbinic tradition in Judaism than of the biblical prophetic and priestly traditions in Judaism.

not to say that study and the acquisition of knowledge were not central to Reform Judaism; but what does seem clear is that the specific mitzvah of *talmud torah lishmah* as mitzvah was not clearly articulated until recent times. Earlier conceptions of Reform Judaism certainly claimed that study was a pathway toward a spiritual encounter with God. Yet in earlier platform statements, the act of study itself was never quite sanctified as a sacred act itself; rather, it was an exercise in each individual's attempt to find God through the written record of past generations' visions of the Divine.

An analysis of the three platform statements of Reform Judaism throughout its history in North America bears out this neglect. Indeed, not one of them contains any specific reference to the mitzvah of *talmud torah* as a commanded or spiritual experience. The Pittsburgh Platform of 1885 remains a document rooted in a faith based on reason. The closest reference one can find to the mitzvah of study is the statement that Jews should "accept as binding only the moral laws and maintain such ceremonies as elevate and sanctify [their] lives."[4] Reflective of the early Reformer's theology on revelation, this statement places primary emphasis on human beings' ability to apprehend God through reason.[5] In the Columbus Platform of 1937, which directly addresses the topic of Torah, we find again the emphasis on the role of human reason in encountering Torah, as opposed to elevating Torah study to a primary position. While we can endorse the sentiment of the Reform Jews meeting in Columbus sixty years ago who wrote, "Each age has the obligation to adapt the teachings of the Torah to its basic needs in consonance with the genius of Judaism," we would search in vain for a more formidable statement on the centrality of Torah study. Under the heading "Religious Life," we find this statement: "The perpetuation of Judaism as a living force depends upon religious knowledge and upon the education of each new generation in our rich cultural and spiritual heritage"—a worthy sentiment but one that fails to empower a practical application.

4: Copies of the three platforms—Pittsburgh in 1885, Columbus in 1937, and San Francisco in 1976—can be found in the appendix to Michael Meyer's *Response to Modernity*.

5: See, for example, Abraham Geiger's Breslau Lectures, 1864–1871. Revelation, he states, "may be interpreted in many ways; but its essence always remains the same—the contact of human reason with the First Cause of all things." From *Abraham Geiger and Liberal Judaism: The Challenge of the Nineteenth Century* (Philadelphia: Jewish Publication Society of America, 1962), 182.

The San Francisco Platform of 1976, otherwise known as the Centenary Perspective, holds that "study is a religious imperative" and that one of a Jew's obligations is to "lifelong study." Purposely vague in order to satisfy a variety of interests in the movement, the San Francisco Platform, like the previous two platforms, lacks a specific mandate for Reform Jews to embrace the mitzvah of *talmud torah*.[6]

With the exception of the passage from Mishnah included in *Gates of Prayer: The New Union Prayerbook*, it took another twenty years after the adoption of the San Francisco Platform for the leadership to respond to the obvious lack of commitment toward *talmud torah lishmah* among Reform Jews. In 1997, UAHC President Eric Yoffie publicly declared there to be a literacy problem among Reform Jews and prescribed as one remedy the specific mitzvah of Torah study. This central mitzvah was at last acknowledged at a gathering of Reform Jewish leadership.

In our own times, solutions to the literacy crisis present special problems and potential pitfalls. First, there is a temptation to apply the latest technology to the task. With all that computers have to offer for study on-line, we run the risk of losing an essential element particularly important to *talmud torah*: face-to-face human interaction. The Talmud tells us, "When two or more sit to study Torah, God dwells among them."[7] And the word used here by tradition is *Shechinah*, the intimate God—not the warrior God of Genesis, *El Shaddai*, or the retributive God of justice we call *Elohim*; not the name for God on High, which is *El Elyon*—the God who is near, at hand, an intimate, loving, and challenging presence, the *Shechinah*. This word is derived from the Hebrew root *sha-chen*, meaning "to abide, to settle down, to dwell, to be a neighbor." Each of these terms may have a very different meaning for us as well.

Learning on-line, we encounter other terms denoting the places of the new virtual reality—*homepage, webpage, chatrooms*—all places one could just as easily imagine existing in both the computer world and

---

6: For an extended discussion of the platform, where a stronger statement is rendered, see Eugene Borowitz's *Reform Judaism Today: What We Believe* (New York: Behrman House, 1983), 142–43. Dr. Borowitz writes that the "Jewish commitment to study is directly related to the religion's major thrust, sanctified living, and so becomes a major religious duty, not a possible option for one's leisure. It is also primarily an adult activity, since the commandments devolve upon them, and only secondarily upon children who study to learn what to do as adults.

7: Attributed to R. Chananya ben Teradyon in B.T., *Avot* 3:3.

the world as we know it away from the screen. But can we encounter the very presence of God, the *Shechinah*, the near and neighboring God, in such settings, virtual spaces fenced off from real human interaction? Robert Frost's words, "Good fences make good neighbors," may be a poetic axiom of our age after all. But surely the rabbis were after something other than fences when they proposed that the *Shechinah* dwells wherever two or more sit together and study words of Torah—in a real room with real pages. In fact, the notion of bringing God from the fiery altar of the central sanctuary and into the house of study, of bringing God from the high heavens above to the holy space surrounding those engaged in study, discussion, and learning, is definitely not about boundaries and fences and borders. God's presence in learning inspires us, even empowers us to break down fences, to push at the borders, to seek out our individual limits and move beyond them, physically, intellectually, and with our souls. We need partners for that, study partners.

Such partnerships, with others and with God, can do much toward alleviating the alienation so many people experience. In place of spiritual disciplines such as meditation or yoga, Judaism offers Torah study as a solution to this spiritual alienation. As described in the *Nefesh ha-Hayyim* by Rabbi Hayyim of Volozhin, a disciple of Rabbi Israel Salanter, we learn that "there is no way to attain the sparks of the light of the soul other than by sacred toil and cogitation and contemplation of the holy Torah. For both [the soul and the Torah] have one source , as the discerning are well aware." [8] Using the kabbalistic notion of Torah study as a vehicle for attaining oneness with God, this rigorous defender of *talmud torah lishmah* claimed that the act of study leads to communion with God. Not through meditation, burning herbs, or incense candles, but the communal act of study. And with all that the worldwide web may have to offer to those whose preferred method of learning is the computer screen, it cannot take the place of studying with another.

So when we refer to study, let us be very clear. We mean interpersonal study. The kind of study that has as its only interactive components the human soul and the human brain, where the screen is not dot matrix but flesh and blood. God exists in the drama of the moment,

---

8: Rabbi Hayyim of Volozhin, *Nefesh ha-Hayyim 4:1*. Quoted in Norman Lamm, Torah Lishmah: Torah for Torah's Sake in the Works of Rabbi Hayyim of Volozhin and His Contemporaries (Hoboken, NJ: Ktav, 1989), 114–15.

as we face one another in all our intelligence and frailty, learning together, breathing the same air, and taking a deep breath before asking
the questions we are afraid to ask, giving the answers we didn't know
were in us, and breaking down walls with new understandings that we
gain in those holy moments suffused with God's presence, because we
chose to study together. When we engage in study via the computer
screen, we run the risk of rendering ourselves cybernetic inhabitants of
Plato's cave, without the light or flickering flame. Alone, echoing over
telephone wires is a world occupied by people unchallenged with the
drama of human interaction. If you don't believe what I am saying,
then try choosing between telling someone you love them and typing
it onto a computer screen; consider how easy it is to hide behind the
unedited flow of words and phrases that course over the lines and elec-
tronic wires. In the face-to-face encounter you cannot hide, for not
only does another dwell directly across from you, but the Other, God,
the Divine Holy Presence, dwells among you as well.

A second obstacle to recovering *talmud torah* are the seductions of
the New Age spirituality movement. This millennialist movement, born
close to the end of the Christian twentieth century, is a false messiah
preying on our yearnings for peace of mind and soundness of body. Acknowledging these needs among all spiritual seekers among us, synagogues and rabbis and organizations and Jewish professionals seek to
attract people with a variety of programs and innovations, but rarely,
until our recent age, with good old-fashioned study. We always have
an *oneg* with plenty of cake and sweet things to eat. We play videos. We
go on retreats. We dance together and sing together. We have workshops on modern *midrash* that have us acting out biblical tales in the-
atrical tights and Capezios. There are meditation classes, prayer sessions
with yoga, and a new term called JUBU, to include Jewish Buddhists.
Some New Age Jews pray with crystals, or burn sage, or chant.

The marketing of these recent manifestations of Judaism is a
patently American phenomenon, an odd manifestation where Madison
Avenue meets a spiritual Jerusalem and a host of Jewish professionals
seeking to market their wares. The marketplace assumes a buyer who
is lost and looking for comfort for self and body, so the market provides
comfort. But is it possible that we are underselling our own most pre-
cious commodity, our treasured relationship with God, to be found in
Torah study? Our tradition suggests that we are.

Rarely do we blink an eye at the cultural admixture of Eastern religious traditions with Jewish religious traditions, if only it keeps people Jewish. But the danger lies not in a dilution of what is authentically Jewish. The cultural hybridization of who we are is part of our story. Indeed, we have borrowed from cultures other than our own throughout the ages. The danger lies in the overemphasis on the self in many of these practices. Torah and the Self. The Body and *Midrash*. Healing and Torah. It is, as Christopher Lasch put it twenty years ago, a culture of narcissism.[9] The contemporary religious seeker desires comfort, oneness, wholeness in this life, as states of being in and of themselves. The Jewish message requires, in exchange for a sense of wholeness and spiritual belonging, something quite different. It does not say that redemption is here—it says we have to bring it. The message does not say that revelation happened once and only once but requires that we consider God's word to be a living word, forever in formation. It does not seek God in the body or embodied in a tree that offers blessed shade but rather implores us to action, to *avodah,* service, in the name of God.

Today's obsession with the self is so strong that we run the risk of losing Jews to their own exuberant need to express themselves, to "actualize" their selves, and to proclaim to the world over and over again their own existence. Like Narcissus, we run the risk of drowning in the reflecting pool of selfhood. And the larger Jewish community runs the risk of losing Judaism's unique communal faith relationship with God.

Directly related to the prevailing culture's emphasis on the self is the desire to validate our Jewishness by telling stories about ourselves. Thus, I would argue, the third pitfall in the road toward fulfilling the mitzvah of classical Torah study is the attempt to construct personal narratives about Jewishness. On the one hand, these personal narratives do serve to root us in an ethno-cultural tradition, adding our names to the pages of history. On the other hand, in telling only of ourselves, we risk severing our Jewish selves from the potential encounter with the Divine to be found in study. I remember, for example, a popular early-morning breakfast club in rabbinical school that was called "Why I Do What I Do." There participants confessed their personal motivation for the performance of mitzvot, ignoring the not-too-subtle definition of the term *mitzvah*—commandment!—where motivation hardly matters. Such exercises may go far in explaining the particulars

9: Christopher Lasch, *The Culture of Narcissism* (New York: Norton, 1978).

of one's Jewishness but ultimately fall short by not accounting primarily for what Judaism demands. Our own stories are a starting point, but they cannot take the place of learning the tradition's stories from an earlier age.

Like many in my own generation, I began with the construction of my own personal narrative in my search for authentic Jewishness. I was raised with very little substantive Jewish religious teaching. My identity was a Jewish identity, albeit a secular Jewish one. Its explanation came by way of my father's army photographs of himself and his friends during World War II, a war that was for him and countless others a righteous war, a Jewish war. This was indeed a unique first encounter for me with the Jewish oral tradition. Like the unwritten legends of Torah in the white spaces between the black letters, those black-and-white photographs and their accompanying stories linked me to my father and to an encounter with the evil forces in Europe. Through photographs, I traced the links between a small town in the province of Minsk, to immigration to America; to the legends of being a first-generation Jew drafted into the U.S. Army; of return from war, the G.I. Bill, college, a career, and a family. These stories rooted me emotionally to a Jewish family and the Jewish people.

From the photographs spread on the floor of the living room, with names attached to the unshaved faces of young soldiers, this narrative moves to a synagogue sanctuary on Rosh Hashanah Eve. I am a small child, sitting beside my father, who is sitting beside his father. The two older generations stumble along in Hebrew. I watch my father's finger, slowly leading the way from right to left at the edge of the page and then back again, impressing me greatly but teaching me nothing. Like many Jews of my generation, I did not receive an inherited tradition of particular Jewish learning. And yet, the claim is made that an oral tradition exists, a Jewish one, one to be learned and then transmitted to the next generation. Stature, economic success, a secular and professional education, and decent moral standards were certainly expected. Religion in general and Judaism in particular did not have to provide them. Where was the voice of tradition for liberal Jews to insure that Torah would be an inheritance learned from one generation to the next?

It was not until college, at the University of Wisconsin–Madison, that I first encountered Torah study. Hillel Director Dr. Irv Saposnik was the first teacher I ever had who offered regular, one-on-one Torah study. Over the course of a year, in his office on Friday mornings, we would read the Book of Genesis, line by line. It was there I became immersed for the first time in a dialogue with the tradition, from early *tannaim* to medievalists to modern biblical critics and poets.

During my junior year in Jerusalem, I searched for a rabbinic mentor. I found Rabbi Hank Skirball, who agreed to weekly sessions. Every encounter left me exiting his office with a pile of books in hand to be read before our next discussion. The command to study was quite real and each assignment fulfilled. As commonplace as these meetings may seem, they were as vital to me as my father's war stories. I was laying the foundation for finally grasping the mitzvah of *talmud torah*. In each place, there was an office filled with books. Here I am reminded of Rashi's comment to Joshua ben Perachyah (in *Avot* 1:6) that "get thee a companion" means that, in addition to a teacher and study partner, one should acquire books![10]

To many secularized, liberal American Jews, the mitzvah of *talmud torah* has until recently meant any kind of education.[11] From the early days of German Reform to the continuation of that educational model here in North America, with the prize possession of young Jews the obtaining of a college degree, liberal Jews have struggled with the concept of the command to study. Much is made in professional circles of "modeling" and "mentoring" as necessary to the development of one's career; but what attention is given to the ethical relationships we learn when engaged in the mitzvah of Torah study with personal teachers?

One thinks of the spiritual heroism of Franz Rosenzweig, whose own journey back toward tradition was most definitively expressed in his views on Jewish learning. Lamenting the "blow" of Emancipation and its potential negative effect on European Jewry, Rosenzweig feared that Jews had abandoned the center of gravity of Jewish existence—

10: *Pirkei Avot* 1:6. See also the *Sayings of the Fathers* edition (London: East and West Library, 1952) with notes and commentary by Rabbi J. H. Hertz, who adds that books are the "best of companions, and invaluable for the acquisition of religious knowledge." (London: East and West Library, 1952).

11: One can trace this phenomenon to intellectual roots in the German Enlightenment. Concepts of secular education as a replacement for religious education can be summarized by the word *bildung,* meaning a faith in the rigors of educational development rooted in individuality, autonomy, and rationality. In his *German Jews beyond Judaism* (Cincinnati: HUC Press, 1985), George Mosse has argued that the key to this concept was the "belief that acquired knowledge would activate the moral imperative." This should be understood as distinct from the Torah tradition's view of acknowledging the commanding voice of God.

talmud torah—for the secular university studies afforded by their new-found freedom. In a speech written for the opening of the Lehrhaus in Frankfurt, Rosenzweig correctly understood the great challenge facing European Jewry, one that still applies to us today. He advocated a new form of learning for Jewish adult education that leads "from the periphery back to the center; from the outside, in."[12]

For our generation of Jewry, highly successful and fully assimilated, Rosenzweig's daring assertion continues to call us home to Jewish study. In study, he argued, will we find the "remembrance" so many alienated Jews of our generation are seeking. In study, one discovers a home for the self in the community. In such a place, Rosenzweig wrote, one is granted the gift of "an inner remembering, a turning from externals to that which is within, a turning that, believe me, will and must become for you returning home. *Turn into yourself, return home to your innermost self and to your innermost life.*"[13]

Like the Israelites who stood at the foot of Mount Sinai and acknowledged God's demand that Israel take up the yoke of the commandments with the words *na'aseh v'nishma*—we will do and we will listen—I was blessed to have a similar experience. My early lessons in the mitzvah of *talmud torah* had as their central component the very act of *doing* Torah study. From the earliest, rudimentary steps into a world of Jewish learning to the sublime experience of worship, I now find myself sitting in synagogue to pray, using the words from Talmud elevating Torah study to a heavenly command. Though this passage was restored to our prayer book more than twenty years ago, the mitzvah of Torah study has now been elevated even higher by the call among the movement's leadership that Reform Jews commit themselves to lifelong Jewish learning. The call is for a lifelong process of Torah learning because it is in such places that Jews seek and find God.

Tradition relates a debate that took place among Rabbi Tarfon, Rabbi Akiba, and Rabbi Jose the Galilean over which aspect of service to God is greater—study or practice. Akiba's answer—that study is greater because it leads to practice—remains the call to all Jewish seekers in our age. The measure of our current leadership's call will depend in no

---

12 "Upon Opening the Jüdisches Lehrhaus," in Franz Rosenzweig, *On Jewish Learning*, Nahum N. Glatzer ed. (New York: Schocken Books, 1955), 98.

13: "On Jewish Learning," in Nahum N. Glatzer ed., *Franz Rosenzweig: His Life and Thought* (New York: Schocken Books, 1953), 228–34.

small part upon the ways we respond to this crisis. In that regard, much can be learned from our early rabbinic ancestors of the first century. These rabbis, perhaps the first to live among a mass of Jews and non-Jews caught up in the whirl of millennialist movements, responded to their crisis of the Temple's destruction by replacing traditional modes of worship with a study-based system of learning and practice. They were concerned not merely with their own spiritual well-being; rather, it was the health and welfare of Jewish life. The fact that we exist two thousand years later as a people is proof that their point was well taken: that through prayer, we uplift our souls. And that through the mitzvah of study—*talmud torah lishmah*—we find the face of God.

Leviat ha-Met
Honoring Our Dead

SUE LEVI ELWELL

We Jews seek holiness in every aspect of our lives and turn to the tradition for maps for our spiritual journeys. Many believe that the elaborate system of mitzvot provides one such map of meaning. Liberal Jews understand mitzvot in many ways. Whether we understand the term *mitzvah* as an opportunity for sanctification or for service, or if we claim mitzvot as religious obligations, many of us also utilize the words that traditionally accompany the act of fulfilling a mitzvah: *"asher kidshanu b'mitzvot."* Some understand these words as thanks to the Holy One for giving us opportunities for holiness by the performance of mitzvot. Others of us understand these words in a more traditional context, thanking God "who has commanded us concerning . . . " for the *ol* or "yoke" of the responsibilities of the obligatory mitzvot. With these words, we celebrate the holiness, claim the obligation, or delight in the opportunity of performing ritual acts such as washing the hands, kindling holiday and festival candles, and celebrating our holy days and festivals.

And yet liberal Jews have cast aside a powerful opportunity to make the mundane holy and transform our relationship to death and loss. The tradition of *hevra kadisha*, the Jewish voluntary society dedicated to *leviat ha-met*, accompanying the dead, calls its members "the holy partnership." Mastering simple traditions of preparing bodies for burial, men and women who become members of a *hevra kadisha* give their time and energy with no expectation of thanks. How can we liberal Jews reclaim and perhaps participate in this opportunity for holiness?

153

Martin Buber suggested a theology of relationship that has been explored and expanded upon by a range of writers and thinkers.[1] For Buber, the essential relationship in each human being's life is with a Thou, an Other who is a subject, not an object. Through relationships of integrity and intention with other human beings, with whom there is dialogue and interchange, each of us can glimpse the possibility of a relationship with the One who is wholly Other, that is, God.

When we view each person's life as a series of such relationships, we gain new perspectives on the traditional mitzvah of *hevra kadisha*.

> In nakedness I emerged from my mother's womb, and naked shall
> I return.
>
> (Job 1:21)

Jewish tradition seeks to mediate the stark reality of human mortality by insuring that we are surrounded by circles of connection throughout our lives. The first circle is the community that gathers for an individual's *b'rit*, *b'rit milah*, or other ceremonies of welcome into the Jewish community. Certainly no baby has control over the relationships that are represented at this initial *simchah* nor at other celebrations of life until well into adulthood, but as we age, we fashion and choose communities of relation. These circles of support that come together in celebration, in commemoration, or in sadness reflect the relationships that each of us has forged in our life.

Jewish tradition is quite clear that when we depart this earth, we do not do so alone. Certainly, the soul's journey is a lonely one, but just as we are welcomed from the moment of our first appearance, Jewish tradition teaches that the body must be accompanied, cared for, and respected until the moment of burial.

In the first decades after World War II, Americans often attempted to distance themselves from death.[2] Large, ornate mausoleums at well-manicured memorial parks were established at a healthy distance from cities and major thoroughfares so that commuters would not be re-

---

1: Martin Buber, *I and Thou*. Many translations are available, including Walter Kaufmann (New York: Scribner's, 1970). See also Isabel Carter Heyward, *The Redemption of God: A Theology of Mutual Relation* (Washington, DC: University Press of America, 1982).

2: Jessica Mitford's popular *American Way of Death* (New york: Fawcett, 1987) documents the excesses that resulted from our attempt to deny death.

minded of death as they traveled to and from work and play.[3] The work of Elisabeth Kubler-Ross and others eased the way for conversations about death and inspired the creation of college courses and adult education programs to encourage young people to confront, rather than avoid, the topic.[4] The current interest in Jewish death customs in general and in establishing *hevrei kadisha* (the plural of *hevra kadisha*) in particular can be attributed to the contemporary revival of interest in Jewish spiritual practices, as well as widespread frustration at the lack of control over so many aspects of modern life and death.[5]

A community that embraces the responsibility of caring for its dead just as it fulfills the responsibility of welcoming new life, celebrating bar and bat mitzvah, and celebrating with those who commit themselves to building a home as a family completes a circle of care. Any theology or belief system that fails to deal with the details of death, any philosophy that neglects issues of right relation—not only with the living but with the dead—reflects a culture that refuses to confront and acknowledge death.

Tradition describes participation in a *hevra kadisha, hesed shel emet,* as a true act of kindness. Why? Because when one participates in a *hevra kadisha,* a voluntary group dedicated to preparing the dead for burial, there are no thanks from the direct recipients of one's kindness and care. The dead do not speak.[6] Rather, we may understand *hesed shel emet* to be the quintessential act of kindness, an act that has the power to transform the doer. Each person who looks death in the face and washes that face with love and respect shows reverence for life and, by extension, for the Source of life. When a parent washes a child with warm suds and words and songs of love, the child is bathed in care, en-

---

3: One notable exception is Hillside Memorial Park in Los Angeles, which overlooks the San Diego Freeway. One acquaintance intentionally chose a plot on the freeway side of the cemetery "so my daughters can wave to me whenever they drive to the airport!"

4: Elisabeth Kubler-Ross *On Death and Dying* (New York: Collier, 1969).

5: The first and catalytic work was Rabbi Arnold Goodman, *A Plain Pine Box* (New York: Ktav, 1981) and the short film of that name that was circulated to congregations and community groups across the country. See also Anne Brener, *Mourning and Mitzvah* (Woodstock, VT: Jewish Lights, 1993); articles by Daniel E. Troy, Margaret Holub, and Debbie Friedman, in Jack Riemer, ed., *Wrestling with the Angel: Jewish Insights on Death and Mourning* (New York: Schocken Books, 1995); and Cy Swartz, "A Reconstructionist *Hevra Kadisha*" and David Zinner, "Resanctifying the Jewish Funeral," in *Reconstructionism Today* (Summer 1997), 4:4

6: Psalms 115:17.

abling her to go forth into the world with a sense of well-being, grace, and strength. When our journey ends, Jewish tradition provides for another, final bathing by loving, competent hands that honor the body that was home to a soul.

Several liberal communities and congregations have convened voluntary *hevrei kadisha* groups to offer this service. While the appendix to this essay addresses the steps toward establishing such a group, I would like to raise several issues that challenge the liberal Jew who considers reclaiming some form of this powerful tradition.

How forming a hevra kadisha *can deepen the Jewish experience of members of a community.*

> Once, when Rabbi Hamnuna came to Daru-Mata, he heard the sound of a funerary bugle and, seeing some people carrying on with their work, said, "Let these people be put under a ban. Is there not a person dead in the town? How dare they go about their regular business affairs?" They told him that there was a *hevra kadisha* in the town. "If so," he replied, "you are permitted to work."
>
> (*Moed Katan* 27b).

This talmudic reference to a *hevra kadisha* reflects the essential communal position of a group of individuals dedicated to fulfilling the mitzvah of *leviat ha-met*, preparing the dead for burial. Following this dictum, *hevrei kadisha* have traditionally been among the first voluntary societies to be created when Jews have established themselves in a new place.

Contemporary liberal Jews have much to gain from considering the establishment of such a group in their communities.

A HEVRA KADISHA *demands Jewish study.* The first step to the establishment of a working *hevra* is the convening of a study group to examine and discuss traditional laws and customs of Jewish burial. (A bibliography is included as an appendix to this chapter.) Initial study should include an exploration of the particular challenges to liberal communities explored below.

The establishment of a HEVRA KADISHA *in a community makes a very strong statement about the essential equality of all members of a community.* Each Jew who is buried by a *hevra kadisha* is treated with equal honor, respect, and care. Each Jew is buried in simple shrouds, *tachrihim.* Each Jew is buried in a simple casket, *aron.*

A liberal HEVRA KADISHA *models the application of traditional Jewish values to a liberal context.* Responsible and creative Reform Jewish practice, while honoring the autonomy of every liberal community, depends on informed choices. Early Reformers assumed that innovators would be knowledgeable about Jewish custom and tradition so that Reform Jews could make informed choices about practice and belief. By choosing to establish a liberal *hevra kadisha,* your community is reclaiming a rich tradition and making it your own.

The existence of a HEVRA KADISHA *in a community enables all members of that community to feel cared for and supported, knowing that they will be treated with kindness and respect when they die.* In addition, existence of a *hevra kadisha* in a community enables every member of that community to contribute to the maintenance of that *hevra kadisha,* insuring that all community members can meet the modest fees for the *aron* and *tachrihim* and any honorarium that the *hevra* must set to enable it to operate.

A HEVRA KADISHA *creates powerful connections between its members.* Because of the intensity and intimacy of the work, and the fact that it is done in silence or in song, members of the *hevra* usually learn to work well together. Most *hevrot* do not welcome one-time participants except under special circumstances, so members become interdependent.[7]

A HEVRA KADISHA *demands building bridges within a community.* If there are no other *hevrei kadisha* in your community, your *hevra* will be providing a needed service to all members of the community. If there are other *hevrei kadisha* in your city, your efforts at networking with them will be richly rewarded. This cooperative work has the power to bring Jews of different traditions together in mutual respect and admiration. Local mortuaries are essential allies in establishing a congregational or

---

7: Margaret Holub, "How Tradition Brought One Community to Life," in Riemer, ed., ,*Wrestling with the Angel,* 96–101.

communal *hevra kadisha*. A Jewish mortuary is always the first choice, as their professionals will be invaluable resources, both for their experience and their access to *aronot, tachrihim,* et cetera. If your community lacks a Jewish mortuary, the local mortician is an especially important contact. Such professionals know that they are most effective when they work with community members, and your growing knowledge and understanding will enhance these professionals' ability to appropriately serve the Jewish community with greater sensitivity. In addition to the professional support and expertise, your group will probably choose to use the mortuary for the site of your *taharot* (preparing the body).[8]

A HEVRA KADISHA *enables individuals with different skills and abilities to participate in the work in different ways.* A *hevra kadisha* needs individuals who can perform basic administrative tasks (contacting volunteers), those who can act as *shomrim* or "watchers" who take turns sitting with the *met* or *meta* (the dead) at the morturary, reciting or reading psalms, and those who do the actual work of *taharah,* the ritual washing and dressing of the body.

Challenges to a liberal sensibility in traditional burial practices. The practices of a traditional *hevra kadisha* incorporate several assumptions that may be difficult for liberal Jews. The theological assumptions of traditional *taharah* are familiar to any Jew who studied the traditional High Holy Day liturgy. Human beings are prone to "sinful" behaviors throughout their lives, and it is possible to "wash away" those sins. During our lifetime, as we are reminded during every High Holy Day period, *teshuvah, tefillah, utzedakah ma'avirin et roah ha-g'zerah:* "repentance, prayer, and acts of justice have the power to avert the evil decree" that would otherwise be levied against those who "miss the mark." Once we have departed from this earth, however, we are no longer capable of performing these acts. The act of *taharah* is considered efficacious for "washing away" sin and transgression.

Rachel Adler's work on *mikveh* may help us to transvalue the waters that are used to perform *taharah* and to understand in a new way the powerful chant *"taharah hi/tahor hu"* repeated by the members of the

---

8: Ibid., 97ff.

hevra as they pour the prescribed amounts of water over the *met*. She writes:

> If purity is the mirroring of God's oneness in human wholeness, it is no less fragile and transitory than humankind itself. Our flesh is gnawed by disease, eroded by age, menaced by human violence and natural disasters. Our minds and our souls are subject to intrusions, exploitations, indignities. We keep breaking or being breached. We keep knitting ourselves together, restoring ourselves, so we can once again reflect God's completeness in our female or male humanity.[9]

If we consider the term *taharah* to mean "whole," pure in its own essence, "reflecting God," we can understand the process as a final washing or cleansing that consecrates this body as now being in a state of perfect rest, "purified" from the bodily invasions and insults of the world.

The final *taharah* has always been understood as a return to an essential state. The soul is given wings even as the physical vessel is returned to the welcoming earth. The *taharah* does not rid the body of impurities but rather prepares the body for its final resting place. The *hevra* members wash the body in lukewarm water, providing a final touch both of human hands and of soothing water before dressing the *met/meta* in *tachrihim*. As the body entered into life from water, so it leaves life in water; as it entered without the weight of deeds and misdeeds, of the life experiences that both enrich and complicate our lives, so each individual can leave the world, lighter, relieved of burdens and responsibilities, closer to God.

Traditional *taharah* prayers also take for granted a hierarchy of the hereafter. Again and again, prayers petition God to welcome the spirit of this departed into the company of the righteous, to enable the departed "to walk with the righteous," et cetera. Liberal Jews may want to interpret such phrases in the broadest possible sense or to reword these prayers or write blessings that open the way to new understand-

---

9: Rachel Adler, "In Your Blood, Live: Re-visions of a Theology of Purity," in *Tikkun* (January/February 1993), 1:41.

ings of righteousness and what it means to have lived an honorable life.

Traditionally, only leaders of the community or those who are known to be scrupulous in their Jewish observance are permitted to serve as members of a *hevra kadisha*. Liberal Communities committed to creating democratic congregations of learners, communities where outreach and inclusion are essential, will want to welcome any who are willing and able to fulfill the demanding responsibilities of membership, regardless of their position, scholarship, or level of Jewish observance.

Who is a Jew? A liberal *hevra kadisha* may want to consider how to expand their understanding of Jewishness both for service on the *hevra kadisha* and for purposes of burial.[10] In a traditional community, a person is considered to be a Jew if he or she has a Jewish mother or has converted to Judaism. Many liberal communities follow the Reform guidelines of patrilineal descent, that is, if a person has one Jewish parent and is raised as a Jew, that person is considered to be a Jew.

Gender differences are very important in traditional *taharah* ceremonies. Not only are there strict traditions of modesty that assign men to care for the bodies of men and women to care for women,[11] but there are differences in the way that the bodies of men and women are treated. After the body is washed and dressed, many traditions include the sprinkling of dust or sand from the Holy Land on particular parts of the body, following the talmudic teaching that earth from the Land of Israel has atoning qualities.[12] For men, the generative organ is an essential site for this dust, and the accompanying recitation makes specific reference to the *b'rit milah*.[13] Liberal *hevrei kadisha* will want to consider whether and how to use both *afar* (dust) and the pottery shards that are sometimes placed on the eyes of the *met*.

10: Cy Swartz relates how one congregation deals with such questions for burial, in "A Reconstructionist *Hevra Kadisha*," in *Reconstructionism Today* (Summer 1997), 4:4.

11: While strict segregation of men and women is traditional, most communities follow the talmudic injunction that if there are no men to perform the requisite tasks, women can complete them. This, of course, assumes that in every community there will always be trained women to fulfill this mitzvah. *Semachot* 13:10, cited by Dov Zlotnick, trans. and ed. *The Tractate "Mourning"* (Semachot) (New Haven: Yale University Press, 1966), 82.

12: *Ketubot* 111a. Alfred Kolatch recommends that the interested reader read S. Y. Agnon "Earth from the Land of Israel," in Gloria Goldreich, *A Treasury of Jewish Literature* (New York: Holt, Rinehart and Winston, 1982); *The Jewish Mourner's Book of Why* (Middle Village, NY: Jonathan David, 1993), 363.

13: E.g., Jewish Sacred Society, 22.

Some traditional *tachrihim* for women include a small apron that is not included in the *tachrihim* for men.[14] Liberal *hevrei kadisha* will want to consider the symbolism of the apron and most probably discard it. Traditionally, observant men are buried in their *tallit,* with one of the fringes cut. If a man is not observant, some purchase a *tallit* specifically for burial. In liberal communities where the custom of wearing a *tallit* has to do with personal practice and not gender, burial customs should reflect that practice.

In fulfilling the mitzvah of *leviat ha-met,* our communities can become healthier and more whole. A community that embraces death as a natural part of life is a healthy community. A community that claims responsibility for its mourners enables healthy grieving and supports those mourners whose journey may lead them, in time, toward service. A community that takes responsibility for its dead reflects a maturity and groundedness that secures the bridge from Jewish past to Jewish future, even as the currents of cultural change swirl around us. A community that supports a *hevra kadisha* recognizes that each of us deserves to return to our Source accompanied by loving hands and hearts.

HaMadrich, the traditional rabbi's manual, includes a prayer for the members of a *hevra kadisha* "before commencing their duties." This amended version reflects the power of the performance of this ancient rite for those who offer their hands and hearts.

> Source of kindness and compassion, whose ways are ways of mercy and truth, you have commanded us to act with loving-kindness and righteousness toward the dead and to engage in their proper burial. Grant us the courage and strength to properly perform this work, this holy task of cleaning and washing the body, dressing the dead in shrouds, and burying the deceased. Guide our hands and hearts as we do this work and enable us to fulfill this commandment of love. Help us to see Your face in the face of the deceased, even as we see You in the faces of those who share this task with us. Source of life and death, be with us now and always.[15]

14: Ibid., 23.

15: Hyman E. Goldin, *HaMadrich: The Rabbi's Guide* (n.p., n.d.) 119. Interpreted and translated by Sue Levi Elwell, with the assistance of Rachel Adler and Yaffa Weisman.

When we can see the holiness in the face of the dead, we can see the holiness in the face of the living. This is indeed the fulfillment of a holy opportunity. Can we reclaim this mitzvah as our own and strengthen our Jews and our Jewish communities through this ancient act of compassion?

Some general guidelines for establishing a liberal hevra kadisha *in your congregation or community*

1. Speak to your rabbi. His/her help as teacher and guide will be important in both the establishment and the maintenance of your group. He or she also may know of others in the congregation and in the community who will be natural partners in the establishment of your *hevra.*

2 Hold a meeting to inform potential members of your interest in establishing a *hevra* in your community. You will need a core of *at least* twenty committed individuals to make your *hevra* viable, and preferably more.

3. Plan to spend several months in study, preparing for your work. During that time, with the help of a trained rabbi or educator, you will study traditional texts and spend time visiting and meeting with professionals at the local funeral home. You may have the opportunity to meet with members of *hevrei kadisha* in your vicinity, or at least to correspond with them. After months of study, you will practice the art of *taharah* and *levishah* (washing and dressing). When you are ready, you will devise regulations and rules for your *hevra* and decide which members of the group will participate in which aspects of the work. You will need members to make telephone calls, to organize and participate in *shmirah* (literally, "guarding" the body of the deceased from the moment of death until burial), *taharah* and *levishah,* and *hotza'at hamitah* and *kevurah* (carrying the body to the grave and interment). Some *hevrei kadisha* also take responsibility for *nehum avelim* (comforting mourners), arrange and/or conduct *shiva minyanim* , and maintain contact with mourners during *sheloshim* (the month following burial) and beyond.

4. Order and assemble the supplies that you will need, which will depend on which aspects of the work your *hevra* chooses to do: *aronot, tachrihim,* earth and/or pottery from Israel. You will want to prepare or acquire guides for the *taharat* and *levishah.* You will

want to check with the mortuary with which you will work for other supplies: buckets, protective gloves and aprons, a *taharah* board, and more.

5. It is quite possible that your *hevra* may have to perform a *taharah* earlier than you had hoped. You will want to use a combination of experienced and new members to insure that the mitzvah is appropriately fulfilled.

6, From the beginning, you will want to plan at least one yearly gathering to bring together members and supporters of your *hevra* for study and to share a festive meal. This will offer an opportunity for members to reaffirm their connection to one another and to the texts that guide them as they do their holy work.

Recommended Reading

Alpert, Rebecca T. *Confronting Mortality and Facing Grief: Jewish Perspectives on Death and Mourning: An Advanced Guide for Adult Study.* Philadelphia: Reconstructionist Rabbinical College, 1997.

Goodman, Arnold M. *A Plain Pine Box: A Return to Simple Jewish Funerals and Eternal Traditions.* New York: Ktav, 1981.

Kolatch, Alfred. *The Jewish Mourner's Book of Why.* Middle Village, NY: Jonathan David, 1993.

Lamm, Maurice. *The Jewish Way in Death and Mourning.* New York: Jonathan David, 1969.

Riemer, Jack, ed. *Wrestling with the Angel: Jewish Insights on Death and Mourning.* New York: Schocken Books, 1995; paperback edition, 1996.

Weiss, Abner. *Death and Bereavement: A Halakhic Guide.* Hoboken, NJ, and New York: Ktav and the Union of Orthodox Jewish Congregations of America, 1991.

Wolfson, Ron. *A Time to Mourn, A Time to Comfort.* New York: Federation of Jewish Men's Clubs, 1993.

Zlotnick, Dov, trans. and ed. *The Tractate "Mourning" (Semachot).* New Haven: Yale University Press, 1966.

cॐ ॐ

Notes on Contributors

RABBI ANDREW N. BACHMAN is the Skirball Director of the Edgar M. Bronfman Center for Jewish Student Life at New York University. Formerly, he served as rabbi–educator at Congregation Beth Elohim in Brooklyn, New York.

RABBI DANIEL M. BRONSTEIN is a program officer/educator at the Jewish Life Network in New York. He is currently a Ph.D. candidate in Jewish History at the Jewish Theological Seminary of America.

RABBI HERBERT BRONSTEIN is senior scholar at North Shore Congregation Israel in Glencoe, Illinois, where he served as senior rabbi for a quarter of a century. Previously, he served as rabbi at Temple Brith Kodesh in Rochester, New York. A member of the Department of Religion at Lake Forest College, he also served as chair of the Liturgy Committee of the CCAR and the Joint Commission on Worship of the CCAR/UAHC. He is the author of the *Passover Haggadah* of the Reform movement, with over a million copies in print.

RABBI SUE LEVI ELWELL first served on a *hevra kadisha* while she was a rabbinical student at Hebrew Union College–Jewish Institute of Religion in Cincinnati. She now lives with her family in Philadelphia and serves as assistant director of the Pennsylvania Council of the Union of American Hebrew Congregations.

RABBI LAWRENCE A. ENGLANDER is rabbi of Solel Congregation of Mississauga, Ontario. A past editor of the *CCAR Journal* and a member of the CCAR Liturgy Committee, he holds a doctorate of Hebrew Letters from HUC-JIR in the fields of Jewish mysticism, rabbinics, and modern Jewish thought.

RABBI ELYSE D. FRISHMAN serves as spiritual leader of Congregation B'nai Jeshurun, The Barnert Temple, in Franklin Lakes, NJ. She is the author of *Haneirot Halalu: These Lights Are Holy*, a Chanukah home prayer book.

RABBI ELYSE GOLDSTEIN is the director and *rosh yeshiva* of Kolel: A Centre for

Liberal Jewish Learning in Canada, a full-time adult education institute of the Canadian Council for Reform Judaism. Her first book, *Re-Visions: Seeing Torah through a Feminist Lens,* was published by Key Porter Books in October 1998.

RABBI NILES E. GOLDSTEIN is a program officer/educator at the Jewish Life Network and an associate of CLAL: The National Jewish Center for Learning and Leadership. A former congregational rabbi in New Rochelle, New York, he is the editor of *Contact* and author of *Forests of the Night: The Fear of God in Early Hasidic Thought* and *Judaism and Spiritual Ethics.*

RABBI PETER S. KNOBEL is senior rabbi at Beth Emet, the Free Synagogue, in Evanston, Illinois. He chairs the CCAR Liturgy Committee, is a member of the Executive Committee of the Joint Commission on Religious Living, a past chairperson of the CCAR Reform Practice Committee, and editor of *Gates of the Seasons: A Guide to the Jewish Year.*

RABBI MICHAEL L. MORGAN was ordained at the Hebrew Union College and received his doctorate in Philosophy from the University of Toronto. He is professor of Philosophy and Jewish Studies at Indiana University in Bloomington, Indiana. He is the author of *Platonic Piety and Dilemmas in Modern Jewish Thought* and editor of *The Jewish Thought of Emil Fackenheim, Classics of Moral and Political Theory,* and *Jewish Philosophers and Jewish Philosophy: Essays by Emil Fackenheim.*

RABBI MICHAEL S. STROH is rabbi of Temple Har Zion in Toronto. He served as president of Arza Canada, chairperson of Arzenu: International Federation of Reform and Progressive Religious Zionists, and co-chairperson of the Reform Roundtable, a discussion group on the content and direction of Reform Judaism. He was an instructor at Queen's College of the City University of New York and the University of Waterloo; he also taught at Hebrew Union College–Jewish Institute of Religion's School of Education and School of Sacred Music.

RABBI ARNOLD JACOB WOLF is rabbi of KAM Isaiah Israel, the oldest Jewish congregation in the Midwest. He is the author of four books and over two hundred articles, a selection of which will be published by Ivan Dee Publishers.

RABBI ERIC H. YOFFIE is president of the Union of American Hebrew Congregations. Since becoming president in June 1996, Rabbi Yoffie has made a return to Torah and the need for increased Jewish literacy his major messages. When he was the director of the Commission on Social Action, he emphasized strengthening the connection between social justice and religious living. He has written widely on Jewish ethics, the Religious Right, Jewish education, and Israel.